soul purpose
FINDING THE COURAGE TO FLY

Krista Emma Gawronski

Transcendent
Publishing

SOUL PURPOSE
Finding the Courage to Fly
By Krista Emma Gawronski

Copyright © 2015. Krista Emma Gawronski
All rights reserved.

No part of this publication may be reproduced, distributed, or transmitted in any form or by any means, including photocopying, recording, or other electronic or mechanical methods, without the prior written permission of the publisher, except in the case of brief quotations embodied in critical reviews and certain other non-commercial uses permitted by copyright law.

First Edition October 2015 OptiMystic Press, Inc.
Second Edition February 2017 Transcendent Publishing
Library of Congress Control Number: 2017934859

Transcendent Publishing
PO Box 66202
St. Pete Beach, FL 33736
www.transcendentpublishing.com
(800) 232-5087

Transcendent
Publishing

Soul Purpose logo design: Lisa Kasch
Photography: Victoria Webb Photography

ISBN-10: 0-615-82649-0
ISBN-13: 978-0-615-82649-3

Printed in the United States of America.

Be Brave with your Life!

DEDICATION

It is with a grateful heart that I dedicate *Soul Purpose* to my family. Thank you for teaching me about love, dedication, and sacrifice. I hope this book fills your heart with joy, peace, and gratitude. To the beautiful women that I have served with, thank you for your dedication to our community and to the Fabulous Women. The pages of this book are filled with your love and positive energy. To my loving husband, Paul, thank you for encouraging me to follow my passion. You are my true love. To my boys, Frank and Vince, I hope this book always reminds you to use your gifts, be true to your heart, and follow your dreams. You, too, shall fly.

With love & Gratitude,
xo

TABLE OF CONTENTS

ACKNOWLEDGEMENTS 1

A MESSAGE FROM THE AUTHOR 5

HELLO BRAVE SOUL 11

FEAR OF FLYING 15

CLEARED FOR TAKE OFF 23

TURBULENCE 25

GROUNDED FOR INSPECTION 31

BAGGAGE CHECK 37

THE CRUMPLED CAPE 45

MAKING TRAVEL PLANS 49

LEAVING THE NEST 55

BIRDS OF A FEATHER 61

FLYING LESSONS 63

LEAP OF FAITH 67

CO-PILOTS AND SOUL MATES 71

EXPLORING NEW POSSIBILITIES 77

CATCHING FIRE &WIND	83
FULL CIRCLE MISSION	89
FLYING IN FABULOUS FORMATION	93
SOARING TO NEW HEIGHTS	103
LEAVE THE KEY UNDER THE MAT	113
THE FLIGHT OF GRATITUDE	119
TO MY SONS	125
ABOUT THE AUTHOR	133

ACKNOWLEDGEMENTS

I feel great pride about the release of *Soul Purpose*. It holds the most sacred part of my soul. It is a tribute to my entire family, the Acevedos and the Gawronskis. I know that my father Armando is smiling down from Heaven as he has always encouraged me to be a leader. I share the love in this book with my brothers, Robert, Armando and Artie. Your peace and happiness matter. I send joy and gratitude to the dearest women in my life, my mother, Gail, and my two sisters, Sylvia and Sandra. Thank you for loving me at all times and supporting my dreams. To my nieces, nephews, and Godchildren, I love you and hope this book touches a new place in your heart. To Ron, Mark, and Scotty, thank you for bringing laughter to our family. We needed that. I gratefully acknowledge my in-laws, Dan and Catherine Gawronski who have treated me like their own daughter and influenced my life greatly. Your unconditional love and support have made me believe that I can do anything that I pour my heart into. I adore you. Sunday dinners have fed my soul.

I would like to acknowledge Oprah Winfrey. She has been a role model in my life since I was a teenager. She challenged me to look inward and realize a greater purpose outside of myself. She was the first person to introduce me to the word **"Soul,"** and she has influenced my philanthropic mission. I hope that Soul Purpose returns a wave of love and compassion back to her heart. I also have gratitude in my heart for three special women, Wanda Henderson, Martha Domont, and Karen Bergin. You have been amazing role models. Thank you for teaching me about perseverance, dedication, and grace.

My heartfelt appreciation goes out to the brave women that I have served with on the Fabulous Women's board, Sandra Fetter, Erin Ascher, Heather Banaszek, Michelle Silva, Kerry Enright, Melissa Becker, Ellen Yant, Valerie Montplaisir, Sharon Medley and Robin Freitas. This group has changed my life. We have moved a few mountains and held some important hands during this journey. I'm proud of our group and everything that we stand for. I also want to thank my nearest and dearest tribe of girlfriends that I like to call my "Soul Sisters." Thank you for potluck dinners, heartfelt talks, wine on the porch, and your unwavering friendship. I'm grateful that we can laugh, pick up where we left off, and just be ourselves.

I would like to acknowledge Kelly Rae Roberts for her inspiration. You encouraged me to cross the finish line and complete this book project. I adore your creativity, your joyful spirit, and optimism. You and I believe in three simple words, "*Love always wins.*" I am also grateful to local friends, Lisa Kasch and Victoria Webb. Thank you for your artistic contributions to *Soul Purpose*. Your creativity and generous spirit moves me.

I want to acknowledge the community that I love so much—Petaluma, California. This is a town that shows up for one another. I feel that love from my awesome staff and customers at Mr. Pickles. I have also felt it in matters of the heart. This is an awesome place to raise my children. Petaluma roots are firmly planted in my life. This leads me to my prayer of peace. Thank you to the strong families that have allowed me to share a part of their hearts in *Soul Purpose*, the Banaszek Family, the Forni Family, the Furbish Family, the Murray Family and the Smith Family. Your stories hold significant meaning in my life. Thank you for teaching me and the rest of the community what courage and compassion really look like.

ACKNOWLEDGEMENTS

I want to thank Connie Gorrell and Shanda Trofe. You entered my life at just the right moment with a life changing opportunity. Thank you for helping me release *Soul Purpose*. Your encouragement was instrumental in following my dream to become an author. We have joy in common and we love to inspire women. That is why the Universe has teamed us up! I love soaring together.

To my husband who knows me better than anyone else. Thanks for teaching me to "lean in." I adore you. Thanks for supporting my passion for charity and writing. You indulged me when I got out of bed at three in the morning to write, and you always seemed to know when I needed a date night to Sugo. Thank you for buying my first laptop and saying, "You can do it." I love us together! To Frank and Vince, you give me inspiration every single day. Being your mom is the proudest role that I have in this world.

Lastly, I acknowledge singer and songwriter, Sammy Hagar. Give to Live has to be one of my all-time favorite songs. It's the perfect anthem for *Soul Purpose*. Thank you for holding peace in one hand and faith in the other. Some words bear repeating. May these lyrics and the message in *Soul Purpose* travel far and wide.

> *If you want love...If you want love...You've got to give a little*
> *If you want faith...You just believe a little*
> *If you want love...If you want peace...Turn your cheek a little*
> *Oh you've got to give...You've got to give...*
> *You've got to give to live.*

KRISTA EMMA GAWRONSKI

A message from the author:

Friends, Family and Fellow Soul Seekers,

Soul Purpose represents my deepest love, values, and intentions for the world. It is my book about seizing our spiritual purpose and creating goodness in our lives. Each of us is on a journey that challenges us to go inward and pull out the greatest life lessons. Every experience shapes us. There are gifts and blessings hidden underneath every obstacle that we face, and every day we are challenged to use our gifts for a charitable purpose.

Who do you want to be in the world? It is a decision of the heart. Designing a life that is centered on love, passion, and fulfillment is a powerful and universal intention. We can all nod our heads and support this vision. We want it for our parents, our children, our friends, and ourselves.

This is my tale of love and kindness to the world. It is a conversation about overcoming fear, realizing our gifts, and giving something back to the world. It is completely up to us to inspire goodness and contribute to the betterment of humanity.

I am not sure how to fully express my appreciation for my life. In some ways this book has become my gift back to the Universe. As strange as it sounds, the pages of this book have been writing themselves for several years. At times, it has been my quiet storm. I had to untangle my emotions and experiences in order to realize my place in the world. After a lot of soul searching and processing, *Soul Purpose* has become the center of my mission, prayers, and gratitude.

There are little special touches throughout this book to remind you of your own amazing grace and profound purpose. From the feather on the front cover, to the chapter titles that represent flight, and the positive hashtags, let this book inspire you to be lighter and more joyful in your daily life. Allow the questions at the end of each chapter to settle into your soul and inspire your own meaningful quest. The feather is a very meaningful symbol for me. As you know, the quill of a feather was the very first treasured pen. From silly diaries to private journals, writing has been a gift in my life. Once I trusted myself to write down my experiences, I began to expand my vision for myself and the community around me.

The feather also ties me back to my passion for The Fabulous Women. This is a non-profit organization that I helped start in 2005. The iconic nest which celebrates the charitable energy of this organization continues to fill my heart. For me it is a celebration of people, stories, and acts of love that have moved through this group. The feather is also the wispy reminder that angels watch over us. I have always said that feathers remind me of my hero, CJ Banaszek. He passed away after a difficult battle with leukemia. He was like a brother to my sons. I was honored to be his friend. Gone but never forgotten, I dedicate the feather you will see throughout this book to him. Young and wise beyond his years, he inspired the world to be *BRAVE* and taught me that our lives are exactly what we make of it. It does not matter our age or the circumstances of our lives, we all have the potential to become great teachers. It is our privilege, and our choice, to use our lives for something good; he was as good as they get.

This book offers a gentle reminder that grace and triumph will often be accompanied by hardship and pain. It will also give you the space to celebrate your personal truth, the power of human kindness, and the beautiful full circle of moments that happen every single day. It is about faith, family, friendship and community. When we take a moment from our busy lives to notice ourselves, nature, people in our lives, and rich experiences unfolding, we can operate more often from a place of love and gratitude. I hope this book can be a companion in your journey as you uncover the blessings of your own story. May the pages ignite your dreams and spark thoughtful movement in your life. This is your time to start soaring and it all begins when you declare your Soul Purpose!

Enjoy the Journey.

With Love and Possibility,
Krista

KRISTA EMMA GAWRONSKI

SOUL PURPOSE

#findingthecouragetofly!

KRISTA EMMA GAWRONSKI

HELLO BRAVE SOUL

When was the last time that you felt excited and fearless about your life? Most great moments happen when we take a risk and open our hearts to the world. Every day we are called on to be *brave* and yet it is a word that we rarely use to describe ourselves. We use it for other people who put their courage and love on the line. We assign that title to heroes who have fought their way through major obstacles or overcome extraordinary odds. It is much easier to recognize the strength and grace of others than to own it for ourselves. While most of us are not shouting it from the mountain tops, we all search for importance in the world. We carry our dreams in one pocket and our courage in the other. Whether we recognize it or not, our journey to live a purposeful life is the bravest mission that we will ever take.

There is no telling exactly how each of our stories will unfold. There is no crystal ball to reveal the future. The only thing that we know for sure is that life will present two things: blessings and obstacles. The positive moments will stretch our hearts and offer the gift of love and gratitude. The hardships will test our strength and remind us just how fragile life can be. Those rocky moments will challenge us to dig deep and draw upon our faith. Although it may be difficult to understand in the moment, everything is serving a higher purpose. That is the space where life lessons are learned and spiritual callings are delivered. Understanding that both possibilities are parts of our journey creates a spiritual wisdom. It is then that we can begin to trust that we are on our perfect path guided by the Universe.

Let us agree that a Brave Soul wakes up and welcomes the morning with the desire to do good and be good. Yes, with each new day we are blessed with an opportunity to step outside our comfort zone, try something new, try something kind, start over, and wipe the slate clean if we need to. We are empowered to deliver some form of love and kindness to people we love and people we do not even know. Whatever happens during the day is entirely up to us. It is just that simple. We get to decide our impact on the world. What an amazing responsibility and blessing! Once we own that power, we start to view our lives with a little more sparkle and clarity.

Every amazing journey begins with a positive mindset declaring, "I am alive. Therefore, I have a significant purpose to fulfill. I am the heroine of this story. I am the captain of this ship. I am the co-creator of this life." If that sounds a bit dramatic, it is! We get one shot to make this life a cherished and meaningful experience.

Who do you want to be in the world? This is a decision of the heart that requires some deep reflection. Let us not delay ourselves from joy or personal fulfilment. Let's not wait until the final seconds of the game when we throw up a shot at the buzzer, or wait until the final stages of life and feel the burden of regret. It is all about what we are creating—right now.

We get to determine the value of our contribution in the world. A positive offering requires compassion and effort. It does not happen by itself, but the personal benefits are tremendous. Positive offerings have amazing spiritual and karmic rewards. Our positive actions create ripples of energy and kindness that spread though our families, our friendships and into our communities. We are all a part of the profound energetic field that flows through the world. We are in charge of our own vibration. It is completely up to us to inspire goodness and contribute to the betterment of humanity. Yes, a Brave Soul trusts that there is a spiritual calling for everyone and they are wise enough to allow others to work at their own speed. There is no concern about doing things perfectly or impressing anyone. It is the understanding that being true to ourselves will unleash our passion and inspire new opportunities and blessings. We must simply remember that the Universe asks for just one thing from us—to use the gifts that we are given to make a positive difference.

Adopting this brave mindset is not as easy as it sounds as we are sometimes tempted to wallow in the past, fixate on things that have not even happened yet, or create distractions in our lives. What if somewhere between our breath and these pages we made a conscious decision to invite even more love and divinity into our lives? I began this book adventure with the foolish idea that we can chase our dreams past the age of forty. Our lives do not end after we raise a few kids or dabble with a career. It seems to me that we are all just getting started on this journey. We are just now stepping into our true selves. I am probably like most of you; I have had the chance to make gross errors in my early twenties, I have messed around with a career, nourished a family, and traveled a bit. I have made some great friends along the way. I am finally in a thoughtful space seeking meaningful connections and personal fulfilment. I am also realizing that people around me are craving that same authenticity in their lives, too.

It feels good to stop, realign our priorities, and create a safe space in which to dream. We are simply never too old to follow the whispers. I recognize the fact that our paths might start in one place, but we should end up on an entirely different road. We may not have the directions or a handbook, but there is great power in following our instincts and trusting the guidance of the Universe. It is then that we may realize our great potential; we can begin to unravel the lessons from our experiences and design a life that is centered on love and service.

It isn't until we have tasted life that we begin to understand the value of relationships and dreams. It isn't until we have truly loved or lost someone that life becomes more meaningful. All of these experiences collectively affirm our growth and significance in the world. The cycle of life reminds us that we will occupy our bodies and the earth for just a short time, and we are all meant to give something back to the world. It may happen for you before the age of forty, but it is the meaningful life experiences that shape our soul and deliver wisdom to our lives. This book is about seizing that calling and channeling that energy into a timeless purpose that can only be our own. I like to call it ***Soul Purpose.***

***Our** Soul Purpose journey begins with the brave realization that we are all here to make a positive contribution to the world. We may not know all the details of how our story will unfold, but we can trust that there is a special plan for each of us. Do you already have a sense of what your spiritual calling might be? What is your passion? What touches your heart and moves you to joy?*

#ADVENTURE

FEAR OF FLYING

For a long time I toyed with the idea that I was going to write a book. I'll admit, I was a little scared of the word *author*. It seemed to suggest that I should have some formal presence, an amazing sense of clarity and gentle poise at all times. I wasn't ready to declare that I had my life all figured out. I wondered how far my voice would carry. I kept getting hung up on the silly idea that I did not look the part. The truth is, on most days, I wear my Converse tennis shoes a funky hat, and a pair of tattered jeans. I thought that if I wanted people to embrace my spiritual message, I would have to somehow abandon my free spirit, change up my style, and hang up all the spontaneous fun that I was having. I was feeling so torn because I knew that I had a story in my heart that I wanted to tell, but I was not giving myself the permission to show every layer of my being; my gypsy soul, my dysfunctional child, my fearless superhero, my wounded warrior, and my playful self.

I kept asking myself, "How are you going to overcome this fear, write this book, and raise the level of excellence, love, and charity in the world?" I began telling myself that I couldn't do it, and I was crazy to think that I could write the next best seller. I dismissed all my crazy daydreams, and believe me, I had some really good ones. There were moments when I would sit outside on my porch, close my eyes, and take in the warmth of the sun. I would imagine *Soul Purpose* completely finished and bound together by the love of a community and a lifetime of lessons. Yes, in my dreams in some way, this book would afford me the opportunity to bring all of my favorite women together; the women that have raised me, supported me, stood with me, and inspired me. My vision included all of my female heroes that inspired courage, Oprah, Kelly Rae Roberts, Ellen, Sarah Ban Breathnach, Martha Beck, Louise Hay, and Marianne Williamson. I didn't have an extravagant vision; I just kept imagining a simple day basking in friendship, talking about life, and sharing laughter…lots and lots of laughter.

I envisioned all of the joyful details. Napa Valley, California would serve as the gorgeous landscape for this encounter. I imagined the most heavenly outdoor experience with these kindred sisters. It would be a day that would not only feed our senses but would also nourish our souls. Underneath the most beautiful oak trees and overlooking a vineyard of fruit, we would share a farm table filled with food and goodness. The charm and simple elegance would spill across the table with sunflowers, gourmet cheese, fruit trays, nuts, rustic bread, homemade olive oil, tapenade, and mixed greens tossed in beautiful ceramic bowls, and mason jars filled with fresh brewed tea, lemon rinds, and sprigs of mint.

I saw each woman with their grateful smiles and warm auras. I heard the sounds of their voices. It was a choir of laughter led by my best friend, Erin. Yes, there was joy and comfort at this table. We would toast each other with vintage wine, breathe in the fragrances of the earth and enjoy the most meaningful conversations about the journey of life. Best of all, that table became a court of love. These women understood the message of my book and they celebrated *Soul Purpose* with me. Though that vision felt delightful, it was a bit out of my reach.

I can now look back and appreciate that girl who was daydreaming on the porch. She was all tangled up and conflicted with fear and optimism, unable to see where her frailty ended and where her courage began. She prayed that *Soul Purpose* would find its way. She felt small next to a very large dream. These were big wishes; the kind that required a field of dandelions. She imagined what it would feel like to pick the perfect dandelion, clench her eyes together, and blow as hard as possible until every last floret was gone and she was left with just a simple stem. Yes, that was me daydreaming on the porch, afraid to spread my wings yet completely hopeful that my spirit would persevere.

It's funny how we sometimes sabotage ourselves with negative messages. At the early stages of writing, I did not trust myself to finish the book. In fact, I seemed to be the only person standing in the way of my dreams. The cynic and the critic would interrupt my writing sessions, and my own resistance would show up and break up the party. A judgmental little voice inside me would say, "Now you just shush! Don't be silly. It's just not going to happen!"

I would often succumb to the doubts, pour myself a glass of Zin, and put away my laptop for weeks at a time. Just like that, my dream to complete *Soul Purpose* and share my charitable message with the world were put away into a dismal wasteland never to be found again.

Each and every time I talked myself out of writing this book, the Universe would conspire and direct me to keep going and stop being afraid. I had to come to terms with the fact that life doesn't show up in some cute little Tiffany box. Rather it is tender and tragic, glorious and unreasonable. It is filled with unpredictable storms and emotional challenges. Yes, I had to embrace the reality that it wasn't always pretty, but every layer of my life gave me new blessings and an awareness. In fact, looking back, it was the toughest moments that reaped the most beautiful rewards. They seemed to disguise themselves as pain and suffering when I was going through them, but they eventually brought me to another level of wisdom and spirituality. I suppose I am sharing this because most rewarding experiences come when we push through a tough experience, fear, personal doubt, or a sabotaging thought.

To write this book meant that I had to let go of the idealism that I had to have everything in my life in just the right place, and I did not have to change myself before I could get started on my dreams. In fact, I began to realize that to fully love myself meant accepting everything; the chaos, the unfinished projects, the milestones, the family secrets, the extra five pounds, the mistakes, the hangovers, and a crap-load of dirty laundry. That moment was an epiphany and it seemed to break open the dam of doubt that I had spent many years creating. Once it opened, ideas began to flow, words began spilling onto pieces of paper all over the house, post-it notes were taped all over the place and chapters began to unfold. I love that moment because I declared that I would become an author and that my dreams were worth fighting for. It was the first time in my life that I took my own hand and said, "You can do it." Best of all, I decided to hold a space in my imagination for that spectacular 'girls day' as I described in Napa with the dearest women in my life and my heroines.

It is so easy to abandon our goals and listen to our insecurities. I am learning that the treasure of wisdom does not lay in the perfect moments. It is, in fact, the emotional hike to the top of our mountain and the incredible lessons that present themselves along the way. The truth is that no one can finish your dreams for you, and I came to the realization that nobody could possibly finish my book but myself. Setting out to accomplish any big dream is going to require guts and determination. It is harnessing every bit of our mental, physical and spiritual self to realize our potential and push through the obstacles. Sometimes the fear of failure and success can be very paralyzing, but the courage to finish is exquisite! I am fairly certain that wisdom comes when we decide to take that risk and when we fully immerse ourselves in the moment. That is when we realize our own true strength and passion. It's letting go of immediate gratification and putting in the actual time and hard work. In a world where *I want it right now* is the common mentality, we are reminded that patience and progress are traits that sustain our character. These helped the turtle win the race and it changed the caterpillar into a beautiful butterfly. It can certainly help realize the dreams that we have all stored at the center of our souls.

We can probably agree that it is way more exciting to actively pursue our dreams than it is to play life safe, otherwise we are letting the current of everyone else take us through life. That is truly less than satisfying. Each of us wants to leave our own unique stamp on the world. We want to have a profound impact and feel a sense of pride and accomplishment. There is a saying that I stumbled upon and absolutely love by Steve Jobs, "People who are crazy enough to think they can change the world, are the ones that do." It is fantastic because it silences the critics and the pessimists. It opens the door to the hopers, the seekers, and the dreamers, and it embraces those who have a remarkable vision to improve the world. Let's face it, these *possibilitarians* don't have an easy go of it. To create change, they have to buck the norm and challenge people to inspect their lives. They will ask us to become a force of truth and kindness despite our adversity and personal suffering. These spiritual leaders sometimes travel a path of resistance and might even appear rebellious to an elder generation that does not always wish to change. After all, most of our parents will swear that they got along just fine without technology, play groups, therapy, and gluten free bread.

With each generation it seems increasingly important to cycle new people into this spiritual role. We need their philosophies and compassionate voices. They are the peacemakers, the healers, the teachers, and the story tellers. They make it their mission to enlighten the world by raising our consciousness and compassion. We lean on these people for wisdom and spiritual direction. They have an ability to find blessings in every situation, and they understand that grace and opportunities are in direct proportion to the energy that we bring into our lives.

Ever since I was a little girl, I felt like I was supposed to do something important. I can't say that I had any idea of what that was supposed to look like—I only know that I could not sit still. It was just a small voice inside me that had big dreams. My father always told me that I needed to be a leader, but in the same breath he would say, "You can't change the world." What a weird burden! I wondered for much of my life why I couldn't just do both. I suppose it took forty years of my life to figure out the answer to that question and stop shushing that little voice inside. *Soul Purpose* began as a quiet internal storm. There was tugging and pulling going on inside me, to be certain. The Universe seemed to be steering me in a new direction and I resisted. It forced me to look inward. It was not until I took the time to untangle my feelings and experience that *Soul Purpose* became a divine message in my life. It has become my mission to raise the level of compassion in the world…not because everything is just right, but because we will all have to overcome some experience or suffering that makes our lives more meaningful. I am very clear that the Universe has orchestrated a journey for each of us. It is up to us to get quiet and realize what amazing possibilities are within our grasp. Our lives become so much more meaningful when we prepare positive intentions.

I know that my heart was assigned a long time ago to lead, gather, connect, heal, listen, inspire, and help people in ways that I could not explain. I have been fortunate to experience great moments of love. People, stories, lessons, tragedies, and victories have moved through me. Those moments deserve a voice and an audience, and it is for that reason this book came to happen. Yes, it will give you pieces of my story, but it will also highlight the phenomenal lessons that have floated to the top. They have helped me strengthen my faith and refine a universal message about discovering our *Soul Purpose*. I hope the pages ahead ignite your own fearless desires and secret talents. May you become a crazy optimist and relish the journey to become exactly who you want to be.

In order to see the amazing possibilities available to us, we must be quiet and reflect on the truth of our lives and face any fears that hold us back from truly living out our passion.

#IMAGINE

KRISTA EMMA GAWRONSKI

CLEARED FOR TAKE OFF

Isn't it amazing when you ask children, "What do you want to be when you grow up?" They always have the most joyful and authentic answers such as astronauts, doctors, teachers, singers, veterinarians, professional athletes. Their answers come straight from the heart. They are not afraid of judgment or giving the wrong answer. Children are just so pure and genuine. It's funny how we become of age and stop asking those questions of one another and ourselves. It seems that the older we get the more challenging it becomes to stretch our thoughts, our wings, and our comfort zone.

How many of us actually still ask ourselves, "What is my calling? What would I do if I wasn't afraid to fail?" It makes me curious as to where the heck all the innocence and child-like wonders disappear to. It is not like we reach a certain age and discover that we have life completely figured out. Are we at risk of getting old and becoming grumpy and complacent? No one wants to wake up one day only to realize that we had let the best days of our lives fall away without capturing a single dream. It is inevitable; all living things will grow and eventually pass away. Time and nature sets in, even if we are not paying attention.

It is completely up to us to decide how we will spiritually evolve. What's it going to be? Are we going to let one season run into the other and one year pile up onto the next? Or will we decide to seize the moment?

Life is calling and the runway is cleared for take-off. The only thing left to do is find the courage to fly.

We wake up every day with the awareness that new experiences and possibilities are available to us, but I wonder how many of us really think about how that transforms into passion, adventure and personal fulfillment. Is it just enough to breathe and let life happen; or do we give ourselves permission to soar? There is so much freedom in those words—*permission to soar*. There is excitement and vibration and it flirts with all of our senses. It is intriguing to think that anything is possible for you and for me. It seems the only permission that really needs to be granted is our own.

How liberating to realize that we have the power to explore our gifts and flourish at whatever we want. Dorothy went on a big adventure to see the Wizard of Oz to figure that out. Must our journey be that dramatic? Do we have to find ourselves in the middle of a swirling tornado or in the midst of chaos in order to realize our power, or can we just trust the rhythm of our lives? It is amazing and true—if we listen close enough to that rhythm we can turn our stories into our messages, and carve out our own amazing *Soul Purpose*.

__Our journey begins when we recognize our gifts and give ourselves permission to follow our dreams. What are three things that you love to do for yourself that bring fulfillment and joy?__

#FREEDOM

TURBULENCE

If you have ever been in an airplane and experienced turbulence, you understand how scary it can be. Turbulence is pocket of disturbance in the wind flow that causes a bumpy effect which can jolt the aircraft and rock you back and forth. It can turn an otherwise smooth mission into a stressful and chaotic situation very quickly. When you are experiencing turbulence you have very little control over what is happening, and it's natural to panic. In fact, it's not usually until you have landed safely on the ground that you can regain composure and a let out a sigh of relief.

While not everyone has experienced flying in a plane during a storm, you can imagine the confusion and chaos it might cause. Sometimes life has a way of knocking the wind out of us, too. Adversity can sock us in the gut when we are not looking. It is an interesting theory to link life and turbulence together, but there is simply no denying it. Life will promise us a few tailspins. Those are vulnerable moments that make us feel as though we are powerless and drowning in fear. How we decide to handle those moments is a critical piece to our journey.

I remember growing up with the old adage, "When life gives you lemons, make lemonade." It sounds simple, right? Well, I suppose it could depend on who you ask. Some people kick and scream when they are confronted with adversity. They run from it, hide from it, and bury themselves in work, alcohol, and denial—whatever it takes to avoid the pain. There is a certain comfort in avoidance, but the Universe is persistent and may beg us to listen and learn. We each have burdens to carry—a difficult childhood, financial worries, a broken marriage, loved ones that are sick, grief, estranged relationships, caring for aging parents, and the list goes on and on. But what if those stupid lemons revealed some divine calling in your life? Now, I know this may be a difficult theory to buy into because life often deals out some of the most unfortunate situations to some of the nicest people. I have seen it on the most personal level. It challenges us to adopt faith and subscribe to the idea that *everything happens for a reason.*

For years I thought that was my personal mantra, but I was quickly humbled and reminded by my hero, CJ Banaszek, that it was not truly mine at all. It is for everyone. CJ grew up across the street from my family. He was like a brother to my sons, Frank and Vince. Our little neighborhood became a nucleus of love. It was comprised of a few families, and all of our children mingled in and out of each other's homes like siblings. When CJ was diagnosed with leukemia at the age of eleven he wrote an amazing passage about having cancer. It was called Everything Happens for a Reason. I can only say that I have never witnessed such grace from another human being than I witnessed from CJ. Wise beyond his years, he poured out honest paragraphs about how bad things can happen in life, but that we should remind ourselves that something good can come of it. Here is one of the incredible passages from his heart.

> *Every day I have one thought in my mind that pops up, 'everything has a reason.' My whole cancer journey could turn into something bigger than anyone could imagine. Someone could get inspired by my story and start a cancer research foundation,*

or make a fundraiser for something like that, or anything. My Bay Kids Studios documentary could be submitted to a film festival or someone could see it and start raising money to let other children have the same school experience in the hospital that I'm having. My point is, even though we have to go through this horrible experience, we will turn it into something brilliant.

—CJ Banaszek

It is a great wonder how a young person could deliver such a profound message. CJ was an old soul who became a town teacher. He captured the heart of the community because he refused to give up, abandon his humor, withdraw his dreams, or let go of hope. His message about courage sparked incredible love in our town. In fact, his spirit and courage took on the moniker **CJ Strong.** The community wore that phrase on car windows, football helmets, tee-shirts and it adorned banners at the local football field. People understood that CJ Strong was a beautiful term of endearment and a badge of honor. Yes, CJ had a warrior spirit that would not quit because life got hard. His poise and optimism taught loved ones and strangers some of the most important lessons of life. While most of us will not have to deal with a life threatening illness as he endured, we have become enlightened by his journey. CJ operated at the highest level of courage and wisdom because he could hold space for the duality of pain and purpose. His life was nothing short of grace.

CJ actually beat cancer. It was a victory that was overshadowed by his passing. The physical wear on his body was just too much, and he lost his life two years after his diagnosis. How does a young boy with a quiet nature step into a very public spotlight and transform the spirit of a town? Well, it was not because he had cancer—it was because he used his adversity to create miracles. He had a divine mission and he fulfilled the promise to turn his hardship into something brilliant. While I'm at it, I don't mind telling you that CJ's entire family became a force of strength throughout his leukemia battle. His mother, Heather, has since embraced this life altering experience by committing herself to be a local representative of Alex's Lemonade Stand Foundation (ALSF). This is an organization that centers its mission on raising awareness, spreading hope, and funding research to find a cure for childhood cancer.

It is a little ironic that I grew up with the saying about turning lemons into lemonade as I now witness close friends carrying that out on a most profound level. CJ's essay about overcoming adversity and orchestrating greatness did not become a passing dream. It was not some silly assignment that was thrown into a memory box with old report cards and art pages from grammar school. No, this beautiful essay became a blueprint of love for his family and a dream to cure cancer. The fact that his family demonstrated a supreme level of courage and dug past their fears and grief to accept CJ's purpose as their own is truly beautiful. It remains one of the most inspiring messages of love that I have ever witnessed. It affirms a very important truth: We do not always choose our destiny, but we may choose the purpose in which we live. Every day I am inspired by CJ. I know that there is not a single thing that I cannot handle because he taught me what it means to be truly brave.

Because a purpose has a divine quality that surrounds it does not mean that everything will always go our way. Our life experiences tell us something quite different. It may, in fact, represent the worst pain of our lives. Perhaps we can look at it from a different perspective. A divine path is spiritual; it stretches our hearts and shrinks our egos. It simply means that we are placed in situations where we can grow to our most profound potential, love at the deepest level, and use our life for some greater good. It is the road less traveled and may require a box of tissues and some humility.

Believe it or not, there is pain and freedom in every difficult passage through which we walk. I am convinced that the most difficult hardships test our faith and perseverance, and those times of darkness deliver amazing blessings, too. We merely have to be open in order to receive them. Those moments teach us how to lean on others and become even more compassionate. They are reminders from the Universe that we are not completely in charge. We are directed to a spiritual path, and it is completely up to us to accept our soul assignment.

I wish that I could say that I have it all figured out, but the truth of the matter is that life, lemons, and lessons are still in progress for me. As a student of life, I am constantly searching for answers to get through this journey with some sort of dignity and grace. Isn't it funny how embracing life means that we have the opportunity to design a beautiful experience, but also run the risk of ending up with a broken heart? Maybe the best way to juggle these dynamics is to let go of our expectations that life must be perfect and realize that turbulence can set in at any time. We must remember that behind each obstacle there may be a larger reason unfolding and the Universe may be nudging us to do something new, perform service, or go in an entirely different direction.

Life is about collaboration, digging in with people, and connecting with them on the most spiritual level. We will all be placed in situations where we will need to show up to support others through their pain. We will also have to learn to ask for people to support us through our own hardships. It is a very fine line between leaning in and leaning out. Humanity is perhaps the most beautiful quality that distinguishes us from other animals on the earth. Human beings are inherently good and our universal language will always be love. I personally believe that the best stories are the ones that allow others to see a little bit of themselves in real-life situations. Maybe that is why we tend to gravitate toward stories of triumph, or cheer for the underdogs to win the big game. We get behind our hometown heroes, and we search for happy endings. Secretly, we are all looking for reinforcement that everything is going to be okay and that the world is innately good.

If there is one thing that you take away from this book, let it be a greater understanding that every part of our lives continues to affirm a calling toward a path of service. Whether it makes sense in the moment or seems completely unfair, the people that we encounter, the burdens, the messy dilemmas, the beautiful moments and even the worst of times, are directing us to our higher purpose. Every tiny piece of it will develop our character and expand our role in the world. The moment that we accept the truth of our lives is the moment that our calling begins.

What has been the most turbulent time for you? Are there any lemons in your life that have created an opportunity for a path of service?

#CJSTRONG

GROUNDED FOR INSPECTION

Most of us are so busy juggling our responsibilities we rarely get a chance to just sit down and enjoy a little quiet time. The term, "I'm so busy" seems to be the standard answer when people exchange pleasantries. There is no doubt that the world is much faster than it used to be. Rather than sit on the sidelines, most of us have decided to try and keep up with the crazy pace. It's go, go, go all the time! We never have to miss a single thing because we have our smart phones, the internet, and a DVR. We have become a society that engages less and less and texts more and more.

Technology and social media have made it super easy to remove ourselves from real life conversations. While our smart phones have added a certain convenience to our lives, they have also created a few more walls between us and meaningful human contact. There have been far too many moments where I have caught myself losing track of a conversation or special experience simply because I was distracted with my phone. In fact, I have found it more challenging to shut everything off and just be silent. I am realizing that it is very easy in this day and age to create a dependency to our phones. Somewhere between our Facebook pages and our Instagram photos we are losing real time and missing an all too important point. There is not a single technological advancement or app on our phone that can replace human interaction, solitude, nature, prayer, or God. Our social media pages, our texting tones, our notification beeps may feed our egos, but they won't address the hunger that lies deep in the soul. In fact, if we are truly serious about developing some deep meaningful calling, we will have to adopt some quiet ritual that requires us to turn off all the distractions, put away our phones away, and sink into a deep breath. That is where the soul sleeps and the Universe speaks.

Most of us know on some level that it would be better for our mind and soul to shut off the noise and get still. American author, Henry David Thoreau, did it in the 1800's. He retreated to the forest to live for several years in order to find his purpose. Of course, not all of us will retreat to Walden Pond to find our truth. It would have to be a much simpler task to make it work in today's world. A little self inspection can put us in touch with our true feelings and our deepest dreams. It is asking ourselves probing questions that truthfully address our wellbeing:

Do I feel balanced, healthy, and fulfilled?
Am I trying to avoid anything or anyone?
Do I feel a sense of purpose in my life?

The only promise that we will need to make with ourselves is to be completely honest with our answers.

It is true, life is extremely demanding for our own good. '*Me time*' can quickly get swallowed up by the daily demands of our career, children, carpools, housework, and figuring out what's for dinner. In fact, most of us are so overscheduled that we don't know what to do with ourselves when a few free hours do happen to fall in our lap. That is why it's more important than ever to find a quiet place to breathe and receive. If we remove the chaos and the clutter for just a little while and develop a pattern of quiet, we will be able to actually hear ourselves and listen to the divine messages that are coming through. It is in our silence that we can let our gratitude flow and allow grace to fill every crevice of our being.

It really was not until I started setting a little time for myself in the morning to write and pray that I came to realize how overscheduled I was and how chaotic I felt inside. I started playing back my conversations with people, and I began to realize that I didn't like what I was hearing. I was becoming a complainer. I would tell my sisters and friends the poor me story, "I'm *so* busy; I am overwhelmed and tired." That wasn't the person that I wanted to be in the world. I didn't realize that I was just excusing myself from being completely present in the moment. It was my way of checking out emotionally and warning others that I may not be able to show up for them, either.

It was very eye opening to realize that though I was being productive and responsible, my behavior was actually isolating. I was also starting to disconnect from my deep feelings and my dreams. Somehow, I had convinced myself that being busy meant that I was important, so I had no real reason to change. I kept telling myself, "You poor thing. You have so many responsibilities." I believed that I was this victim of circumstance. I had no say in the matter, and I was too exhausted to see any other way to be in the world. Ironically, when I started to get quiet, chapters started to unfold in this book, and I began to get clear on my purpose and my spiritual direction. I realized that I had complete choice in where I was putting my time. I could pick and choose my activities, the people with whom I would spend time, and how busy I wanted to be.

If our quest is to go deeper in our lives then we must bring some quiet practice to our lives. It means that we are willing to ask ourselves important questions about our emotional, spiritual, and physical wellbeing. This must be an honest ritual that evaluates what is working and what is not working in our lives. It is truly an act of kindness that we give to ourselves. It is proactive love. We don't have to wait for a crisis to occur or a meltdown to happen. It should happen simply because we love ourselves enough to check in. If you think about it, we do this lovingly with friends all the time. We call them to see how they are and catch up on their joy, their health, and their activities. It's funny how it seems to be such a difficult task to give ourselves the same love and consideration. We have gotten way too comfortable as a society staying above the surface. It is becoming increasingly clear that we all need to go deeper if we want to have more authentic exchanges. Our truth and our grace settle just below the surface and it patiently waits for us to invite it into our daily practice.

So, where do we find the quiet space to reflect? It will be different for everyone. It might be a moment in the garden, a hot shower in the morning, a pot of tea in the afternoon, a visit to church, a run after work, or a little prayer before bed. It has to be something that is doable and preferably enjoyable. Just because yoga works for one person does not mean it will work for another. It is consciously going inward because we know that life has deep spiritual rewards, and our access to our divinity can only reveal itself in a quiet space.

Making that spiritual shift in our lives is hard because we start to take responsibility for ourselves on a whole new level. It means taking an emotional inventory and acknowledging all parts of our character—the good, the bad, the ugly. When we get to this place, we must remember be kind to ourselves. After all, we each have the potential to be little reckless, broken, overscheduled, quirky and imperfect at times, but we also have an amazing potential to be wise, graceful, useful, loving, and extraordinary.

GROUNDED FOR INSPECTION

Where do you find your quiet space for reflection? How do the external distractions get in the way from making a deeper connection with yourself and others? What meditative routine would you like to invite into your life?

#QUIET

KRISTA EMMA GAWRONSKI

BAGGAGE CHECK

There is much freedom in self-acceptance and letting go of the need to be perfect. As much as we would like to have it all together all the time, it is just not possible to attain such a high standard. Sometimes life gets a little complicated and messy. It's nothing that we should feel ashamed of or embarrassed about. If we are seeking our personal truth, we can put away all the different masks we hide behind and just love ourselves for who we are. I can honestly look back at my life and see some vivid moments when I was trying to convince myself and others that everything in my life was just right. I strived for perfection, and when I came up short, I was pretty hard on myself. It was exhausting to keep up appearances, and I had unachievable lists running in my mind relentlessly. I seemed to be wearing a mask all of the time. I just was not willing to give myself permission to make mistakes. I have since realized that in order to be right, I would find some justification in making someone else feel wrong. Also, in holding myself to a ridiculous standard, I only hurt myself and my health. For a very long time I was in a vicious cycle of chasing perfectionism. I had insane pressure to be in control at all times, and it was propelling me in the wrong direction.

I have often pondered where that pressure for perfection originated. Was it growing up with the dysfunction of an alcoholic home? I now know that it was part of the reason. That little girl inside me thought if I did everything right, I could diffuse the tension in my home. I believed that it would make everything better. What I did not realize is how that behavior would carry over into every part of my life. As an adult it was interesting to come to terms with my codependent behavior. I realized that it did not stop just because I moved out of the house. The need for control became habitual. I put the same pressure on myself at school, at work, in my marriage and when I became a mother. Though I was in a different environment, I still held myself to an unreasonable standard. Was I trying to deem myself worthy of love? Was it just the fact that I am a woman and I am constantly trying to live up to the demands of my family and expectations of society? I suppose it all played some part in my madness.

There is a funny story that comes to mind that speaks to this insanity. It remains a favorite story of mine simply because my fifteen year old, Frank, had to set me straight and teach me a valuable lesson about letting go. Now, I probably have about twenty boxes in the attic that are labeled *Christmas.* Each year it has become a bigger production to pull out all the stuff. When the kids were little, I enjoyed creating little scenes around the house. There were Christmas memories everywhere. Every ornament and snow globe had a story. As the kids have gotten older, I have noticed that I am still the only one pulling out the Christmas stuff. Sure, it is always beautiful when it's all up, but what a stress case I became in trying to create a winter wonderland. It wasn't until I was challenged to "let go" by my fifteen year old that I truly understood just how ridiculous and obsessive I could get. He showed me that there is a cost in trying to make everything perfect. I can lose myself in the process.

Here is how our exchange went: It was after Christmas. It was a rainy day in January and I was out on the porch putting away all the Christmas decorations. My neighbor, Heather, pulled up in front of the house and said, "Hey, finally putting away the Christmas stuff, huh?" This was the same neighbor that had the discipline to put her decorations away the day after Christmas. I laughed and told her that I was waiting for the Epiphany to take it all down. In that moment, I swear I was twelve and proclaiming all my Catholic School knowledge about the three kings bringing gifts to Baby Jesus. She laughed, fully knowing that I had a lot of crap to put away, and the Epiphany was just a solid excuse for dragging out the clean-up.

I asked my son, Frank, to come outside and help. He watched me untangle all the cords and harness every rusty reindeer into their waterproof bags. I was soaked. My Christmas parka that had a furry hood looked like a dead cat wrapped around my face. Frank looked at me and said, "Mom, why do you do this to yourself every year?" I stopped what I was doing and told him that I thought it made everyone happy. He informed me that I did not have to work so hard; I could simplify everything, and they would be much happier because they could see me enjoy myself more. I couldn't believe it, my boy had just caught me mistreating myself. I thought to myself, "When did he grow up? Where have I been?" I did not have to pretend there was a Santa Claus and according to him, I did not have to put so much pressure on myself either. I looked at Frank and said, "Thank you...thank you so much!" With that, I proceeded to pick up every reindeer and launch it off my porch into the middle of the street. People driving by were alarmed. No longer was I Santa's Helper, I was a reckless housewife that had just been liberated by her fifteen year old son. With every single reindeer hurled into the air I became lighter and more joyful. I was laughing so hard that I was crying. Imagine my relief.

My boy understood the need to simplify. He called me out. He was telling me to be kinder to myself and let go of stuff. I hugged him and thanked him. And just like that, it was me that had the Epiphany that day—*less is more and perfectionism is completely over-rated.*

Motherhood has a way of teaching us phenomenal lessons about what is important and what is not. It has taught me to worry less and trust more. It helped me come face to face with the big taboo word called, *control,* and to make a concerted effort to surrender more, be forgiving, trust myself, and find peace in my faith. Once I figured out that I did not have to put so much pressure on myself to be perfect, life has gotten much easier. Oh, I am not completely reformed, but I feel much more patient and I have become kinder to myself and to others. I have come to the realization that I don't have to be *right* all the time, and I don't have to be ashamed of mistakes or failures along the way. They do not determine my self-worth. In fact, I finally understood that those less than perfect moments are good for the soul. This is when the Universe hand delivers some of the best wisdom.

After spending a lot of time with women over the years, I have seen how we tend to carry the weight of the world on our shoulders. I know that women feel great pressure to get everything done and keep all the balls up in the air. Somewhere along the way, we have adopted a crazy unattainable version of being a super woman. For most of us the pressure is so thick, we are running ourselves down. Somehow, we have to reclaim ourselves. Perhaps, finding humor in my reindeer story will remind us to be a little kinder to ourselves. Let's not hold ourselves to such a ridiculous standard that we cannot enjoy the little things, laugh out loud at ourselves, or see the beauty of our less than perfect situations. It is true, sometimes we have to crack ourselves wide open and be vulnerable to appreciate the most important life lessons.

Silly errors are forgivable and unavoidable. Most of us have blown the punch line to a joke, walked out of the house with two socks that didn't match, received a parking ticket, failed at something, a test, a job, or a relationship. Let us remind ourselves that mistakes are an inevitable part of our journey and we are building awesome character along the way.

We do not have to punish ourselves every day because there was a moment in our lives that fell below expectations. I think that we can agree that it becomes much more difficult to travel on our journey if we are carrying heavy baggage. Let's check in a few bags, shall we? Remove the weight of the world from our shoulders and focus on the things that we do have control over. There isn't a single thing that we can do to change the past. We can beat ourselves up over it, hold onto anger, *or* we can say thank you and gently move forward.

When we make a conscious decision to let go, we can free our energy to focus on all the things that we can influence, like our passion and our dreams. It is liberating and healing for us to acknowledge those feelings that hide below the surface. Hard experiences and difficult people come into our lives simply to teach us more about ourselves. The sooner we learn to make peace with people that have wronged us and tough moments that have hurt us, the sooner we can get on with our journey.

The most fascinating soul seekers are the people who explore their spirituality while maintaining their unique style. I absolutely love when I hear someone say, "They are so down to earth." It is such a nice term of endearment. There is respect and admiration for people who seek excellence and stay true to themselves. While 'normal' is subjective, there is something very beautiful about people who strive for goodness while maintaining their humility. We are much more likely to listen and relate to people who are grounded and have a sense of humor. It's true, the human spirit does not respond to proper punctuation and perfection. It delights in the truth and all the delicious details of life that are real, funny, courageous, naughty, and loving.

I have often thought about my own interesting tale. Life has been anything but dull. I am convinced that my story is engaging for the sheer fact that I am surrounded by a cast of crazy and infectious characters. These are the people that have driven me crazy one moment and melted my heart the next. Oh sure, there are quiet normal ones in the bunch, but there are a few 'holics,' too. It should not come as a complete surprise. After all, everyone has one tucked away somewhere neatly in their life. These are people that drink too much, shop too much, collect too much, eat too much, gamble too much, complain too much, love too much, smoke too much, talk too much, and give too much.

Heaven knows I have done my share of over-indulging, binging, super-sizing and people pleasing. I have had some grand moments of channeling Renée Zellweger as Bridget Jones. Remember her? She was a lovable character because she was passionate and irreverent. She was determined to have some importance in the world despite her dysfunctional habits and a diary filled with mistakes. I love how she could embrace her imperfections and still maintain her amazing love affair with life. My favorite clip in the movie has to be the last scene when she stood in the middle of the street in her leopard print underwear, hugging her leading man, Colin Firth, in the snow.

I can still hear the song from by Van Morrison called *Someone Like You*. That movie gave me goose bumps and permission to laugh about myself. I started to daydream about happy endings. It made me realize that happiness does not have to look a certain way; it does not rely on a perfect family, a perfect job, a perfect dog, perfect panty, or a perfect self. It comes down to attitude, gratitude, and self love. Let's remember that our Soul Purpose depends on a few things: giving ourselves permission to get quiet, allowing ourselves to own our feelings and our experiences, keeping a sense of humor, and periodically getting rid of some old baggage.

Think about something heavy that you are carrying around. It may be time to let it go or say goodbye. By simply recognizing that someone or something came into your life to teach you a little more about yourself marks the beginning of peace and true wisdom. There may be some experience in your past that needs forgiveness. Place your love, acceptance and humor where it is needed.

#SURRENDER

KRISTA EMMA GAWRONSKI

THE CRUMPLED CAPE

At age 45 I don't pretend to have everything figured out. I have realized that gathering wisdom is a lifelong process for all of us. By keeping an open heart and creating space for life lessons, we will continuously invite blessings into our lives. That is not always easy, as our ego wants to appear masterful. If we ponder our life experience, I think we can all find some core beliefs and values that are nonnegotiable. These life lessons are based on our experience of the world thus far, and they ground us in our decision making process. We may have learned them from our trusted circle of friends and family or maybe we had to find them out the hard way. Regardless, I think it is helpful to take a moment to review our personal truths and celebrate the wisdom that is already guiding us through our *Soul Purpose* journey.

It has taken most of my life and a few hard knocks to figure out the toughest spiritual lessons. I begin with the most important, self realization. The opportunities and grace that come into our lives are in direct proportion to the energy that we bring. Whatever effort and good vibes we bring to our family, our job, our friendships and our community will be matched accordingly. I know that passion goes a long way, and kindness really does change the world. It has very little to do with monetary giving. These gifts are exclusive to the heart.

> ♡ I have learned that comparing ourselves to others can only damage our spirit. It is much

more empowering to focus on the gifts that we have and how we are going to use them to make a difference in the world.

♡ There will be times in our lives when we are challenged to be the student and other times when we are empowered to be a teacher. It is important to distinguish between listening to your life and finding your voice.

♡ Goodness is all around us, but there will be situations that test our nerves, challenge our hearts, and knock us down. Consider these people and moments your great teachers. For every positive person you encounter in the world, there is another waiting in the wing to stir up your emotions and present an incredible life lesson. We must remember that we are not defined by painful moments in our history, but rather by the strength of our character and our willingness to love right this very minute.

♡ At our core we all desire the same things: Love, Happiness, Connectedness, and Humanity. Our own fear and ego can create separation and get in the way of realizing our commonality. We will have a better life if we assume the best in others and concentrate on traits of goodness.

♡ Everyone needs a community in which to belong and to fall back on. You can call it a tribe, a family, a book club, a congregation, a soul circle, a sisterhood, an army, a brotherhood or a team. Call it whatever you like, but it is essential to have a safe place to be yourself, find support, seek honest counsel, and exchange energy. There is something very powerful in knowing that *we are in this together*. The people with whom we share shadows should have our back and insist on bringing out our best.

♡ We all have good days and bad days. Neither of them last forever. For that reason, we should not get too attached to things or outcomes. Life runs through cycles of happiness, disappointments, and major life lessons. We will be hurt, tested, and liberated. That is why it is important to learn how to say, "Thank you; I'm sorry; I forgive you and I love you."

♡ Believing in something bigger than ourselves is essential to staying grounded. I often refer to my guiding Spirit as, *God* or *the Universe*. You might call it something else. In times of need or times of splendor, it is good to offer a prayer of strength or gratitude. Faith delivers trust and beautiful assurance that everything will be okay.

♡ Life is meant to be shared. Friendship is the finest gift that we can have and offer in return. There is nothing better than sitting on the porch and talking with a good friend who will mirror the truth back to you, celebrate your successes and pick you up when you feel broken. Whether a sisterhood or brotherhood, our friendships give us a safe place to fall and soar.

♡ It is tempting to get caught up in superficial activities such as gossip, drama, and judgmental storytelling. All of these are ego based conversations that distract us from being authentic and compassionate.

♡ It is much more gratifying to think about what we can give back to the world than what we can take from it. Sacrifice and charity are as much for the *giver* as they are for the *receiver*.

♡ I like to think that everybody has a super hero cape crumpled up at the bottom of their drawer or in their suitcase. Occasionally, we will need to pull it out and be brave even when we don't want to. Life will continuously test our courage, priorities, and sense of humor. I am pretty sure that those moments are meant to keep us humble.

♡ There are four powerful words that every spouse, parent, child, and friend long to hear and feel in the depth of their hearts: ***I believe in you.***

♡ The obsession to be perfect can have exhausting effects on the spirit. Mistakes are a part of our journey. Regret and life lessons simply teach us to move forward in our lives with greater consideration, more integrity and extra love for others and ourselves.

Take a moment to think about your core beliefs. These are the principles that steer you through your journey. What are some positive non-negotiable values that you hold dear to your life?

#BELIEVE

energy to an old wound. When we affirm pain, we deny ourselves joy. As you can imagine, it becomes very difficult to hold a space for both. This is when we are challenged to draw upon our courage and seek positive ways to move forward.

Even if this was not your experience, it is good to understand those feelings, because there are many wounded souls that you will surely encounter in the world. People are still walking around the planet feeling inadequate, unlovable, unsure, and not good enough. They may not realize that their habitual storytelling relinquishes them from having any power or choices in their lives.

This is why it is so important to know where you stand. We are the only ones who can unravel the lessons that our parents came here to teach us. It allows for us to assert our independence. It is important to check in and ask ourselves if the story that we are carrying around supports our emotional wellbeing. Does it allow for our dreams and love to be fluid, or does it in some way limit our growth and potential? There is no right or wrong answer. However, that information will be very useful in gauging the type of energy that you are putting out into the world.

For some people looking back at their history is just too tough, and they can't or won't go there. Let me assure you that it is not about reliving the pain. It's about releasing it and letting go of old messages that have become counter-productive to living our best life. Those who are carrying the burden of guilt, pain, anger, or shame are much more likely to make choices that sabotage their joy and overall physical wellbeing.

After I went to college, I studied the Rosen Method for a few years. It is a form of body work that incorporates breath work and the physical validation of tension. Perhaps the most important thing I learned is that unresolved feelings and life experiences become trapped energy in our bodies. They are internal wounds that affect our psyche. If we ignore them, it becomes tension in our bodies and stress in our lives. It is an unconscious holding that will disrupt the flow of breath. We all know that breath is life, and when we find ourselves holding in our feelings it translates to holding back in some way in the world, or holding on for dear life.

Most experiences that threaten our safety or emotional wellbeing send us into a survival mode. There is no judgment. It just happens. It is self-preservation. We are so determined to just get through it that we forget to give ourselves permission to actually feel. That emotional deprivation will eventually fight its way to the surface. It might show up unconsciously in our decision making or addictive behaviors, it may reveal itself as trust issues, it could be the reason for building emotional walls, or in extreme cases, it may manifest into physical ailments or alterations in our posture.

As you can see, it is important to our spiritual and physical wellbeing to recognize our inner voice. When we stop talking about all the bad experiences from our past, we can step into our present power and start living our best life. Call it a sweet surrender of the heart. It will make all the difference in claiming our purpose. It is a gift when we can come out from under our parent's wing and forge our own journey. While our parents hold a big role in our lives, we eventually get big enough to stand on our own two feet and take charge of our own lives.

Life has an incredible way of coming full circle, and we get to decide how our experience will shape us. We absolutely have a choice in the matter. We can shut down or open our hearts to the amazing possibilities that surround us. We make a choice to walk through light or dwell in darkness.

I am reminded of my father-in-law, Dan. He had a childhood that was pretty tough. He had a stepfather who was an alcoholic and physically abusive. It was a turbulent situation that most people would find difficult to overcome. At the tender age of sixteen everything changed. While Dan's stepfather was working, Dan got into a car with his mother and six-year-old brother and left. They drove across the United States seeking a new beginning. Although it was his mother's courageous idea to leave her abuser, Dan also made a powerful decision. He created a new story for himself. Sometimes I listen to his early childhood reflections and wonder how in the world he found the strength to get away and carve out a new identity. Then I realize that he chose not to be a victim of the past. Instead of repeating the cycle of addiction and abuse, he was going to use the lessons from his stepfather to create a life based on tenderness and family values. I love that story because Dan showed great perseverance. I love how he defied the odds and fought for a healthy environment. He is truly one of the kindest human beings that I have ever met. I am proud to call him my friend and father-in-law.

The sooner we realize that painful lessons are a part our journey, the easier our life becomes. Our suffering does not have to define us. Our parents are part of our story but ultimately, it is up to us to create bold adventures and carve out a new identity. I am convinced that it doesn't matter if there was an abundance of love or absence of love, we have a certain obligation to ourselves to uncover the wisdom that our parents came here to teach us. Make no mistake about it. The Universe was very deliberate about choosing the parents we have. Whether our parents are presently involved in our lives, they have passed away, they are across the state, they are down the block, they are in the hospital, they have disowned us, or they call us every day, there is an undeniable magnetic pull that we feel toward our parents. No matter our age, we have energy tied to our parents' love, their trust, and their acceptance.

We sometimes forget that there is no owner's manual for parenting. It is true that some people make horrible decisions on behalf of their children, but I believe that most people try to do their best with the tools that they have. I suppose we could over dramatize our lives about how our parents screwed everything up, but the truth is, somewhere along the way, we become mature enough and wise enough to make our own life decisions. We must be responsible for creating our own travel plans and generating our excitement about life. I hope you will agree that traveling with a purpose requires a much deeper mindset. It requires faith, focus, and a fearless passion for love. Oh yes, love is all we need. Our destiny depends on it.

What are your feelings about love? Are you comfortable with your expression of love? Do you say it? Do you show it? How have you internalized your parents' energy around love? What are some of the greatest lessons that you have learned from your mother, father, or the parental figure in your life?

#TEACHER

LEAVING THE NEST

If you were to ask me who had the biggest impact on my spirit, I always come back to my parents. They were married at age seventeen and had six children. I was the last one. It was a blessing to be the baby in a big family. My parents worked super hard to raise six children and put us through catholic schools. My dad was my hero, my champion, and my thorn, and my mother was my rock and my faith keeper. I often reflect on my story and think about the most important lessons that I learned from my own childhood. I have come to realize that the hardest experiences have turned out to be the greatest gifts in my life. Now that's something that I did not figure out right away. In fact, it wasn't until I peeled back the layers of my onion that I really understood the nature of my purpose.

If you were to ask me a few years ago about what my book was going to look like, I would have said that it was some documentation of my childhood. It was going to be an autobiography that addressed the perils of alcoholism, but the more I thought about it the more uncomfortable I became with that premise. I began to realize that the story that I really wanted to tell wasn't just about codependent survival. I wanted to talk about the deep rooted love that lives in every tough dysfunctional situation that involves family. It is difficult to understand where the blessings are in the moment, but everything is serving a higher purpose.

I knew that my father's alcoholism was only part of

my story, but the triumphant message was his values and work ethic, my mother's faith and dedication, and the love that grew despite the rough patches. The strongest messages that came from my mother and father were to be a leader, be a thinker, be a person of faith, and be myself. These were the lessons that sparked my philanthropic mission and a *Soul Purpose*.

It became increasingly clear that I wanted to take my book in a different direction and I began to pray about it. I had hoped that some amazing epiphany would direct me on where to go next. I knew that I did not want to write a gloomy memoir. I wanted to highlight the beautiful gifts that camouflage themselves in hard experiences. I also knew that it wasn't just my family that had difficult problems to overcome. In fact, I don't know a single family that has not had to overcome some episode of pain. I knew that love, forgiveness, and perseverance are the common threads that link our experiences, and I was committed to telling that story above anything else.

How was that possible? How was I going to sort through all the tangled layers? Love isn't complicated, but sometimes people are. My parents overcame so much. They taught me amazing lessons about sacrifice. They taught me that true love means sticking around for everything—the joy, the grief, the sickness, the plans for the future, and the unexpected hardships. Yes, my upbringing taught me that life also has a way of coming full circle. If we don't take a moment to review our lives, including the messy parts of our story, it becomes heavy. It begins to feel like a weighted vest hidden under our clothes every day. Ignoring our feelings creates armour and it takes a toll on our hearts, our relationships, and our physical wellbeing.

The Universe must have known my urgency because I was blessed with the greatest gift that I could ever receive—forgiveness. For several years I watched my father physically decline. Life was catching up to him. It was hard to see him slow down, but it paled in comparison to the emotional strain that I felt when I watched him on his final days. He came face to face with his life and I got to feel his love on a completely different level. I held his vulnerability for the first time and really understood the depth of his heart. He had some regret. I know that he wished that he had done a few things differently. He wanted to give so much and carry out a few more dreams. He couldn't speak, but the room was filled with massive love. It was palpable. I wanted so desperately to let him know that he was my biggest hero and my teacher. I prayed that I could reach him spiritually.

I held my dad's hand a lot during those last few days, probably more than I had ever done in my whole life. He held on for as long as he could. With each breath, he seemed to be solidifying his love for us while preparing for his final goodbye. It was difficult to see his struggle between holding on and letting go. He was being called to Heaven, but he fought like hell to stay back. It was clear to me that he had so much more that he wanted to say and to accomplish.

I will never forget the final moments that I had with my father. It was the night before Easter, a little after 11p.m. My family stayed very close to him. We decided to step out of the room for a moment to talk a strategy for comfort. Before I left the room, I took a moment with him by myself. I kissed his forehead. I whispered in his ear, "I love you, Papa. It's okay. You can let go now." I turned on a little quiet night light and walked out of the room. I left unaware that his final breath would be taken minutes later. I wasn't ready for him to go. That was the toughest and most beautiful experience that I have ever gone through. A part of my damaged soul left with him. In that moment I understood that he did the very best that he could, and his love never wavered one bit.

That experience was a blessing because I realized in that moment that we all have a choice on what we decide to hold on to. Our past experiences teach us amazing lessons about ourselves, how to love, how to forgive, and how to persevere. There is love and freedom that comes from letting go. No one can rush it or force it. It's an internal process that we must figure out for ourselves. We can't rewrite the hard parts of our past. We can only walk away a little bit stronger and wiser, and the longer we tell the negative stories we actually prevent positive energy from flowing into our lives.

There will always be things in our lives that we wish were different, but dwelling on things that we can't change will only cause a bitter residue. We can easily get stuck on the disappointment and the disillusionment. That's why it is best to find the goodness and the life lessons. Love is not always transparent. It may require deeper inspection. Sometimes it hides below the surface waiting for just the right moment to emerge. If we can remind ourselves that family dynamics are sometimes complicated and sometimes people have a hard time expressing themselves, then we may just save ourselves some grief. We can come to peaceful conclusions and look to the future with hope and optimism. Let us remember that our peace becomes our practice, and eventually we will all leave the nest and fly on our own.

LEAVING THE NEST

What story do you carry around about your upbringing? What are some positive memories that you have about your younger years? Is there anything from your childhood or your relationship with your parents that weighs heavily on your heart? Take a moment to validate your feelings and offer yourself a message of love and peace.

#PEACE

KRISTA EMMA GAWRONSKI

BIRDS OF A FEATHER

Twenty years ago I was moved to my core when I read the book *Simple Abundance* by Sarah Ban Breathnach. This chapter is my tribute to her courage and her brave message to seek spiritual depth. I fell in love with her passage called The Secret Garden where she presented a deep analogy between tending our lives and tending a garden. In her passage, she talks about a dream and coming to terms with two realities, the dark, dismal wasteland that reflects thoughts of lack and the beautiful landscape that reflects joy, gratitude and abundance. I loved it because it made me realize that we all have a choice on which one we will cultivate in our lives. For years I have thought about that beautiful metaphor and have expanded that idea further in my mind and heart.

I integrated her message into my spiritual awareness in this way. Before we are even old enough to tend our garden, seeds are planted by people who love us. Some of those early seedlings take root and create a foundation. Those are the anchors that keep us grounded throughout our lives and give us a sense of belonging. As we get older, we start to play in our garden and invite people to join us. As the seasons unfold color erupts in the flower beds and joy and gratitude spill over the path. This beauty represents the goodness and the people in our lives that grace us with love and positive energy. Amidst the pleasing flowers, there are tangled weeds that bully their way through. Sometimes they shoot up without reason or warning. These represent the stressful moments, the chaos, and the difficult hardships that occur in our lives. These are the situations and people who come into our lives and teach us lessons about our strength and personal will. They remind us to keep a box of tools handy at all times. We will find it necessary to cut back on the things that do not serve our best interest. We clip back the dead vines and pull out the unwanted weeds. If they are left alone, they grow recklessly and overtake the yard. Eventually, they can overshadow the beauty, stifle the joy and choke away the gratitude.

Thanks to the amazing imagery and the thoughtful words of *Simple Abundance*, I have enjoyed the wisdom of the secret garden for close to twenty years. It is a profound metaphor for living that deserves a new audience. It empowers us to maintain balance in our lives and decide what we are willing to nurture. Nature is synonymous with time and seasons. We cannot rush the growth. Nourishing a beautiful garden means developing maturity and allowing beauty and wisdom to unfold slowly. As the keeper of our garden, we are meant to create a vibrant and peaceful landscape that makes our heart happy. With that responsibility, we must be willing to roll up our sleeves and sort through the rough patches and pull out the dreaded weeds. That is nature and life at its best. It will be glorious one moment and challenging the next.

Take a moment to reflect on your garden. Be willing to see it with complete honesty and without judgment. What are some of the areas that are thriving and blooming? What are the parts of your garden that need your attention and love?

#BLOOM

FLYING LESSONS

The clarity that I pretend to have now was completely absent during my teen years. I think I barely survived puberty, partying, and the fashion disasters of the 80s that included neon and leather fringe. It was a time for mistakes, hard lessons, and the double sided cassette tape of the Eagles' Hotel California. I was a little out of control. I tempted fate a few times, kissed a few frogs and ran a few mucks before I could claim some personal boundaries for myself. Looking back, I danced on an edge. I suppose my life could have spiraled because I was on the fast track. I was rebellious and attracted to danger, alcohol, terrible boyfriends, and some drama. Fortunately, the best thing I had going for me was that I had a good family that I did not want to disappoint, friends that had my back, and believe it or not, I had The Oprah Winfrey Show.

    I could hear faint whispers from the Universe. That little voice inside me kept asking for more from myself. I was longing for priorities, maturity, and a path to call my own. I would like to think that my teenage years marked a period of learning and experimentation that were necessary to figure out who I wanted to be and who I did not want to be in the world. Thankfully, I had a cool routine that was my saving grace during high school. I would religiously record The Oprah Winfrey Show at 4:00 p.m. every day. I remember watching her on the show and loving how she challenged people with compassionate topics and real life issues. I loved the sound of her voice and her life changing messages. There was no false pretense. Her show was a safe place to land, and it continuously challenged me to wake up.

At a time when I needed it most, Oprah had a great topic on her show that addressed taking a personal inventory. She addressed the need for self examination and personal acceptance. She invited the world to learn to love the full length mirror. I have to say that I have thought about that many times in my life. Even back then, I knew that she was talking about something far deeper than vanity. I still think about the relevance of that episode today. Just think about how often we stand in front of a mirror. We do it every day, but how often do we really look beyond our physical selves. Most of the time we stand in judgment picking ourselves apart, wishing for younger boobs, smoother skin, and a flattened tummy. We spend hours brushing, combing, picking, hiding, plucking, smoothing, styling, and moisturizing. At what point do we stop hiding ourselves and appreciate our age, our bodies, our mistakes, and our story? I suppose it is a lifelong lesson for each of us.

For some terrible reason our society has confused worth with physical beauty. It is tragic that a few wrinkles and grey hairs can, in some way, depreciate the value of our lives. Isn't it true that authentic beauty lies deep within our soul? Isn't it true that depth and character carry more weight than a nice bust line or soft skin? Isn't it also true that we all must go through real dramatic life experiences before we can acquire the most profound wisdom? That is why a hug from a grandparent feels so warm and genuine. Years of love and life lessons pour through their arms and their words. Let's remember that we are the only ones that can truly define our beauty and worth. No one else should be entitled to do that for us.

Learning to love ourselves exactly as we are is perhaps the most important act of love that we will ever express. To look in a full length mirror and say, "I love you—period," may in fact be the most liberating statement that we ever say to ourselves. Our love cannot be contingent on being skinnier, prettier, smarter, richer, or sexier; it is cherishing ourselves exactly as we are. That's it—nothing more! Yes, it is time to quiet the critical voices that make us feel inadequate or not good enough.

The full length mirror reminds us to stay in the moment. It will not reflect the past or tell us the future. It simply captures who we are now. Perhaps that's why standing in front of a full length mirror is such a powerful experience. We need to love ourselves before we can ask others to love us too. It has nothing to do with age, money, or status and it has everything to do with our souls. Our challenge is to let go of any pressure and idealism to be perfect. At the start of each day we have to be able to confidently look in the mirror and say, "I trust you and I got you."

Oprah's challenge to look inward started a series of changes in my life. I fondly look back at her show and see how she has been a mentor in my life. I love that this is how the Universe works sometimes. Some people will come into our lives to teach us hard lessons. Others will gift us the treasured wisdom from their own *Soul Purpose* journey. It certainly opens the door to the philosophy that we are not only meant to be the student—eventually we are meant to step into the role of the teacher.

When we look in the mirror, let us promise to say something kind and loving to ourselves. Let us only nurture positive messages. Has there been someone or something that has come into your life at just the right time to teach you an important lesson? What was the lesson and how did this divine moment become a blessing in your life?

#TRUST

LEAP OF FAITH

It is hard to say what marks true adulthood. Is it age, the right to vote, the right to drink, or some internal shift that invites responsibility and soul searching into our lives? There is a point when we should all start to ponder the bigger picture, our future, and our spiritual purpose. Looking back, my college years were marked with bold moves and life changing moments. I was paying way more attention to strong women and positive role models in my life. My sisters, Sylvia and Sandy, were carving out successful careers, and my mother, Gail, continued her mission to hold our family together. They modeled responsibility and I was craving some purpose too. I just wasn't sure on what it was supposed to look like. I started to question which career path to take, and for the first time in my life I actually started soul searching. I began pondering questions that had depth and relevance such as what am I born to do? What am I good at? How can I make a positive impact on the world? That was a refreshing time because I was actually starting to plant seeds for a new vision. I was giving myself permission to live beyond the moment and realize that I had a larger potential outside of surviving my childhood. It was a huge epiphany because I realized that I did not need to rely on someone else to carry me through life. I was good to go! I didn't have to sit on the sidelines feeling afraid. Sure, I had to recognize that there would be no lifeguard on duty and I was in charge of my own emotional safety, but I was ready for adult swim. It felt a little like turning on a switch. There was no looking back. I had finally understood that the Universe had a unique plan just for me.

When I look back at that time, I recognize that there was another woman placed in my life to show me what courage looked like. She had a tremendous impact on my spirit. She was one of those people that had grace and love pouring out of her at all times. Her name was Wanda. Wanda Henderson lived around the corner from our family. Several of her children and grandkids matched up in age to my brothers and sisters, so we spent a lot of time at her house. When I was a little girl, I used to love watching her. She seemed to do everything in her kitchen. She rolled her platinum colored hair in curlers, she prepared lunches and dinner meals for the children, and she would chat with friends at the kitchen table. I loved to listen to her. The kitchen was her command post. She had her phone, an ashtray, and her Braille cards positioned in the same place all the time. She also had her faithful dog lying by her feet. It was not uncommon to see her sitting at that table with her husband Lloyd, or one of her daughters, Linda, Sandy, or Kelli Jo. She held company all the time. She loved to listen to people talk about their joy. If you told her about a dance that you went to, she would ask you to describe your dress. If you got a new haircut she would ask to feel the length. Yes, Wanda was genuine with her listening. She made you feel so special all of the time.

When I was in grammar school I can remember seeing Wanda at my school. She would sit in the hallway and listen to the children practice their reading. She was a Lady Shriner and volunteered at the Lions Club. Wanda was passionate about working with guide dogs. It might seem to be a strange thing to say, but I often forgot that Wanda was blind. She traveled throughout the neighborhood with so much poise and confidence. She operated her life from a place of gratitude and joy.

She modeled courage in a way that I had never seen before. Yes, at a very early age I knew that she was amazing and God had a special plan for her.

At fifteen years old, I went to work for Wanda and her husband Lloyd. They owned a little sandwich cafe in downtown San Francisco. It was called L&W Smoke Shop. It was situated on the 32nd floor of the Tishman Building, a huge skyscraper in downtown San Francisco in the financial district. My time there was short but it had a great impact on my soul. For one summer I had the chance to observe and learn from Wanda. I walked to her house in the morning and we would take the L-Taravel streetcar downtown. She was pretty brave. We traveled on the busiest streets and rode public transportation with people who were tense and stressed to get to work. She had no signs of fear. In fact, she was extremely friendly to everyone she met. She continued her magic at work. On occasion she ran the register. People would tell her what they had. "Hi Wanda, I have a chicken salad sandwich, an apple, and a coke." She would ring them up, exchange pleasantries, count out their change, and send them on their merry way. Yes, it was pretty special to see how she interacted with the world. She taught me to smile regardless of personal obstacles and showed me that we can all give something back to the world.

Whether it was because of my two older sisters, my mom, or Wanda, I was starting to expand my vision for myself. I became adventurous with my thinking, and I realized that no one can hold us back from truly living out our joy except ourselves. We can make the choice to sit out or jump in. We can stay cooped up in our homes or we can go meet new people; we can pick up a book or take a class, or we can stay on our couch and hide from new ideas. It takes a leap of faith and trust in our guidance to expand our presence in the world.

The Universe wants us to become explorers. It's just going to take a little guts and determination.

Is there a defining moment in your life when you began to look at the world with a much broader vision? Give yourself permission to get quiet and clarify your **Soul Purpose.** *What is your life calling you to do? Take a piece of paper and write down the following question: What would I do if I knew I could not fail?*

#EXPLORE

CO-PILOTS
AND SOUL MATES

Part of our *Soul Purpose* journey is discovering who we are and leaving our stamp of kindness on the world. It's taking brave steps to explore our identity and use our life for a greater good. That mission does not have to change just because we decide to share our life with someone. In fact, our spiritual journey is as much for our loved ones as it is for ourselves. When we are actively following our heart's desire and giving back in some charitable way, we are much happier. There is an ease and trust that life is exactly as it should be. Instead of feeling as though there is something missing or that we are deprived in some way, we can feel content and appreciate the goodness that already surrounds us. When we align our gifts with our heart and our passion with our purpose, the Universe will take it from there.

Some of us may elect to travel on our journey alone while others will choose a companion. Whatever we decide for ourselves, we will have to remember that our own joy and fulfillment comes from within. It is not the job of our loved ones to make us happy or fill up all of our time. A partnership is really about sharing ourselves and enhancing our lives. The moment that we need another person to feel a sense of purpose, we have lost ourselves. It is our individual gifts that determine our path. That is why it's important to maintain our truth and independence within our relationships. To be able to recognize one another as a separate soul within a relationship is gift. It is rewarding to have a partner that understands our need to explore and express our passion. If the goal of being together is to bring out the very best in one another, then both people have to recognize the privilege that comes from helping the person you love carry out their dreams.

It is not only good for the heart, it is good for the world. It is another level of unselfish love where two people agree to come together to share passion, decisions, dreams, emotions, responsibilities, and possibly parenting. Creating healthy boundaries means that there is enough space to allow each person to grow and flourish outside of the other. It is an amazing expression of love, trust, and faith. While some people might fear losing their partner's love or attention, it actually tends to have the opposite effect. Space and encouragement are perhaps the most loving gifts that we can give to one another. To recognize that each of us is our own person and we have our own destiny to fulfill is quite amazing.

Of course, these awesome lessons did not reveal themselves until much later in my life. All of my boundaries were misplaced in high school and most of my college years. I gravitated toward the wrong guys. They each seemed to fit the same profile. They partied too much and they were noncommittal. I was so busy trying to fix them, I couldn't possibly consider exploring any larger purpose for myself. I often operated from a place of fear. I always seemed to be afraid of losing a boyfriend, and my self-worth seemed to be determined by the relationship I was in. It was a time in my life when I felt unlovable and I had many insecurities. Anxiety around my home life seemed to carry over to my relationships. I felt lost and broken. It took a few unhealthy relationships, a reckless trip to Mexico, and a pattern of self neglect to realize that I needed to change. I looked at myself in the mirror and I wasn't very proud of who I was becoming. It was then that I decided to require more from myself. I began setting boundaries for myself. Slowly, I adjusted my codependent behavior around men, and I started to view myself as a deserving individual of love.

It is funny how life works. It was when I wasn't looking for love that the Universe led me to Paul Gawronski. He was my older brother's friend. He was cute and as far as I knew, he was completely off limits. After all, you don't just go around dating your older brother's friends. It would be too awkward and weird. Well, fate had other plans and a beautiful courtship began. For the first time in my dating career the relationship was not about changing or saving a man. It was a mutual relationship that allowed each of us to be ourselves and grow. It was a foreign feeling, but I actually liked the person that I was when I was with Paul. I had not seen this girl before. I was happy and self-confident. Once I completely gave in to his laugh and blue eyes, I have never let him go. It took one date to an Elvis impersonator and a seafood buffet to realize that he was the man that I was going to marry. We laughed, we danced, and we talked about dreams. It was a moment in my life when I had an incredible epiphany about relationships. I was never supposed to fix anyone but myself. After a five year courtship, Paul and I joined our lives together in marriage. It was clear that he was my soul mate and he was going to be my co-pilot on this journey.

Marriage has taught me so much. Perhaps, the most important thing I have learned is that we don't have to sacrifice ourselves and our individual passion in order to make a marriage work. There is a balance between holding on and letting go. Giving ourselves to someone does not mean losing ourselves; it is choosing someone that will respect our need to find ourselves. Marriage is definitely an adventure, and you quickly start to realize that 'leaving the seat up' is a very small problem. The bigger hurdles are going to be communication, parenting, working through unexpected problems together, and leaving space for each other to grow.

I am often reminded of the wisdom that my mother gave me on my wedding day. It is a lesson that has saved me from having petty arguments and made me a bit more patient within my own marriage. It was June 18, 1994, and we were in the limo on our way to St. Gabriel's Church to get married. My mother was holding my hand. I asked her, "What is the best advice that you can offer me about marriage?" She took a deep breath. I think her life passed before her eyes—six kids, 12,000 bag lunches, four houses, Girl Scout camp, family counseling, 22 rescue dogs, rummage sales, sacrifices, two bowling teams, AA meetings, sleepless nights, and an insane amount of patience and love. She whispered, "Don't measure." She elaborated as she could tell that I needed more. "There will always be a lot of demands on you because you will be a mother one day. You will have sleepless nights with your babies, chores to do, dinner to prepare and many sacrifices, but it's all worth it. There will be things that you can't do that your husband will help with. That is a gift too. Recognize his strengths and yours. There is an ebb and flow. Just try your best to support and love each other." I melted just a bit. I loved her honesty and I could tell that she was delivering a huge secret that could only be understood through years of devotion and hard work. Marriage was not always easy for my parents, but I could feel those words pouring through her heart. Her legacy will always be her dedication to her marriage, her children and her profound faith. She let me hold that in my hand for a while during that car ride. I will never forget it.

I still take a deep breath and let the wisdom of those words settle in. That was the best advice because it understands that while there is a partnership, there will be moments that we hold each other and release each other. There will be times that one partner is strong and the other is vulnerable and it is not a pity contest about who does more. There will be moments of greatness and frustration. It's choosing which battles to have and validating the goodness and contribution of our partner. Most importantly, it's realizing that our *Soul Purpose* journey continues even though we are sharing our lives with someone. I like to joke a bit and relate it back to being a kid. We may be all grown up, but secretly we still want someone to ask us how our day was, tell us that we did a really good job, and then fix us a cheese sandwich. Yup, marriage is another place in our lives that we seek harmony, a better understanding of ourselves, and create a support system for our dreams.

Our copilots in our journey may be a spouse, partner, family member, neighbor, mentor, or friend. Identify your current support system in your life. Who is the closest person that celebrates your dreams? To receive the maximum support for our vision we have to feel safe to declare our purpose. Finish this statement: I know that deep in my soul that I was born to: _____. When the time feels right, share it with your loved one.

#CHERISH

EXPLORING NEW POSSIBILITIES

English writer and poet, J.R.R. Tolkien wrote in his book *The Fellowship of the Ring* a poem in which he states, "All that is gold does not glitter." I am also inspired by the line in the poem that reads, "Not all who wander are lost." What an awesome tribute to those who are unafraid to explore their truth and passion. To be an explorer means that you are willing to step outside of your comfort zone, seek new ideas, meet new people, and humble yourself to a calling that is greater than yourself. It is true that we generally live up to our own expectations. If we spend a lot of time fearing change and or thinking about our limitations, we will literally never get off the ground.

Our *Soul Purpose* mission begins with a vision to improve ourselves and contribute toward the betterment of the world. Granting ourselves permission to get started is essential. Our success can be largely determined by how well we marry our heart to our mission; we place our faith in ourselves, and put time and energy into our dreams. We must see ourselves as worthy human beings and recognize that we have something beautiful to offer. It's time to defy gravity and any negative messages that hold us down. If somewhere on your journey you were told that you were not good enough, not smart enough, not creative enough, not skinny enough or not brave enough, it is now time to replace those thoughts of being ineffectual, with positive messages. Self love begins with affirming messages.

Remember the childhood story, The Little Engine That Could? We can do anything that we set out to accomplish. I think we can all agree that it is far more empowering to say, "I am beautiful, I am smart, I am caring, I am creative, I am brave, I am timeless, I am the right size, and I have everything I need to carry out my life with joy and grace."

As a woman, it is particularly challenging to claim time for ourselves. Our nature is geared toward taking care of others. Many wonderful women in the world will give, give, and give until they have nothing left to give. If this sounds familiar, hold on. There's more! How many times have we heard friends say that they are waiting for their life to slow down before they sign up for a class, get back to the gym, write that perfect novel, or travel? Everything seems to hinge on their kids growing up, their spouse's schedule, or the classic line, 'when life settles down.' The truth is, we have to make ourselves a priority. It's time to stop loving others at the expense of ourselves. If we wait too long to follow our heart's desire, resentment will kick in, years will pass, and we will lose our passion. We will get stuck on the couch watching reality TV wondering why others are having so much fun.

I recall a conversation that I had with my friend, Sarah. I asked her if she wanted to sign up for an inspirational workshop with me. Her answer touched me. She said, "It has been so long since I have taken any time for myself. My world has been all about my children. My youngest son is now getting ready for college, and I don't even know who I am anymore." Wow! I really appreciated her honesty. I sat with that for a while, and realized that we all want the best for our children. It is super tempting to put all of our energy into them and forget about our own desires. We sometimes think our destiny is tied to our children or our partners, but it's just not true. They are a part of our legacy, but our true calling comes from deep within our soul. Sarah was ready for something to shift in her life. She was realizing that she had stifled her passion and creativity and she had neglected a part of herself for a very long time. That workshop had significant timing. It would give her a symbolic start in the renewal of her spirit. I told Sarah to consider giving herself just one day to refresh her thoughts and her energy. I let her know that a space would be waiting for her. I was really proud of Sarah when she decided to attend. On the day of the workshop, I watched her from across the room. She had a sparkle about her that I had never seen before. I think she woke up a part of her soul that day. I got the distinct feeling that things were going to be different from now on in her life. There was no more denying who she was meant to be in the world, and I had this joyful feeling in my heart for her.

It is true that today's women have huge burdens to carry. We still feel the pressure to keep our homes up like June Cleaver, and we are driven to uphold the progressive ideas that affirm equality, charity, volunteerism, environmentalism, and feminism of today. Now throw in carpool, laundry, grocery shopping, and creating a dinner menu, and all of the sudden life gets a little hairy! It is a tall bill for all of us. How are we supposed to do it all and still keep our sanity and our true sense of purpose? I suppose we have to take a moment and decide what validates our core values and makes us happy. We all can't be activists. We all can't become Mother Teresa or Gloria Steinem. We will each have to create and meet the potential of that one woman that stands in front of the full length mirror every day.

Though we are somehow expected to do it all, we must remember that the greatest leaders in the world eventually narrow down their passion and their dreams. We have to take a moment to look at our lives, our gifts, and our surrounding support system to figure out our *Soul Purpose*.

In general, women find it difficult to acknowledge the hunger they feel deep in their souls. We have gotten a little too used to denying ourselves joy and opportunity. How dare we ask for more when we are already blessed with a family, friendships, and a career? Let's face it, any deeper hunger that rumbles beneath the surface has nothing to do with lack of gratitude. That hunger usually means that some part of our spirit needs to be fed. It is not uncommon for women to nourish everyone else and forget about our own gifts and dreams. We must remember that putting everyone else in front of ourselves does not necessarily serve our family any better. In fact, showing our spouses and our children that we love ourselves enough to value our passion is a tremendous example. They will learn two very important things—they are not the center of the universe and their support and encouragement are important gifts that they can give to their loved ones.

Let's agree that declaring our *Soul Purpose* is not about being selfish. As long as our loved ones are safe and cared for, we can incorporate small changes into our daily routine. It will certainly have to make sense for our lives. You wouldn't want to sign up for a class when you have a newborn at home, but it may make sense to do this later when the kids are in school. It's tough to commit a little reading time in the late afternoon when we have to get dinner plans together, but it may make sense to wake up an hour earlier in the morning and savor a little quiet space before everyone wakes up. We just have to make ourselves a priority and bring celebration to our lives. What if I told you that every day is special occasion simply because you are here? Would it make a meaningful difference? Would you stop putting yourself on the back burner and start doing things that you love?

If you will indulge me for a moment, consider life is a large stake poker game. Imagine yourself sitting at a high profile table surrounded by the most prestigious players in the world. You have a mountain of black chips sitting in front of you. Poised and confident, you survey the other players. In your heart you know that you are just as keen and deserving as anyone else to pull off the biggest victory of your life. Some of the game is the luck of the flop, but success is largely determined by our courage and willingness to play. There will be risk and consequence, but watching from the sidelines will not be enough. Fear keeps people on the sidelines. They might enjoy the peripheral energy, but they can only imagine what it feels like to play at the big table and be in the middle of all the action. You slowly peek at your two cards and see the two beautiful pocket aces. You lay your cards face down, take a slow, deep breath and consider the possibilities. You have amazing cards, but it is no guarantee that you will win. The only thing that matters in that moment is your guts and courage to stand up, push the whole stack of chips to the middle of the table, and declare, "I'm all in!" Are you wondering how that hand played out? Do you find yourself wrapped up in the intensity of that moment? You can decide how that story ends. My larger point is that most of us are walking around with pocket aces. Those are the God given gifts that make us special and bring us emotional victories. The truth is most of us are simply unaware of how smart, creative, funny, and amazing we really are. We have gotten too comfortable just being a part of the crowd, and we have decided that we are not worthy enough to be high powered players in life. At what point do we say, "I want to play...and I'm all in?"

Learning to balance our lives will always be a challenge, but it is time to get in the game. Let's become mentally and physically prepared to carry out our destiny. Physically we may need more rest, more exercise, more water, and more fruits and vegetables. Emotionally we may need something much more profound, more love, more joy, more passion, or more peace. It is entirely up to us to create momentum in our lives. I am reminded of the wise practice that fuels our journey and restores our heart. Let us remember to take what we need. As long as we are putting positive energy into ourselves, we are growing and nourishing new possibilities for our lives. Not every minute will be perfect, but it's all about the moments and the progress. That is why the timeless message from Ralph Waldo Emerson seems to resonate with the world, "Life is a journey, not a destination." This is your life, Sister, and this is your time!

Soul Purpose *will challenge us to explore beyond our comfort zone. By making ourselves a priority we are also teaching others to honor their gifts and their spiritual calling. What are a few specific things that you can incorporate into your day that celebrates passion and honors your purpose?*

#PERMISSION

CATCHING FIRE & WIND

The term, 'Catching Fire' will always remind me of the iconic character, Katniss Everdeen, from the book The Hunger Games. She was brave and fearless. Katniss stood for peace and she defied unbelievable odds to survive. While it was an unimaginable tale of fiction that highlighted both torture and victory in the same story, I walked away from that series wanting some of her fierce energy. I thought to myself, "I want to live my life with that same kind of passion. I want to stand up for truth, love, and blaze a movement that means something." It would take some time and thoughtful energy, but I slowly started to believe that I could do something powerful and meaningful in the world.

It is interesting to compare the person that I was in my teens to the woman that I am now. I was not a huge fan of the girl that stumbled through her adolescence. She needed to experience life a little bit, learn a few tough lessons, kiss a few frogs, and become a little more humble. I now understand that growing pains are inevitable and we eventually gain a deeper perspective about life. Maturity can only happen with time and experience. After I got married and started having children, I started to look at life with a long term vision instead of a short term gratification. My ideas of the world changed. I held myself to a greater standard. I wasn't just going to take; I wanted to *give* something back and be a good example to my children. I became much more aware of people and their compassionate qualities. I began to realize that there was a difference between surviving and truly thriving.

Coming from a large family, I learned at an early age about the concept of sharing the load. It meant dividing the chores, the problems and the last piece of dessert in the house. It was all a part of the framework that my parents created to make our household work. They modeled sacrifice in such a way that I quickly understood its necessity. Throughout my entire life, I have anchored my heart to an important concept: *We are in this together.* It is no coincidence that the very same values needed to take care of our families are what we also need to take care of our communities. If we look closely at our world, we will see that society often has a difficult time keeping its priorities straight. Free will can get us into trouble sometimes. We will always have a choice between two paths, the path that is driven by the ego that asks what's in it for me, or the path that quietly calls on the heart saying, "This is for the greater good."

Isn't it true that we all have the tendency to get caught up in ourselves sometimes? Humans will always battle between right and wrong and be conflicted by needs, wants, and desires. The truth is, sometimes the ego wins, but when we understand that there is always a choice, we become much smarter and thoughtful about our decisions.

As I get older, I am realizing that sacrifice is built on love and it is a necessary to our survival and our humanity. It is the fabric that holds communities together and keeps people united and grounded. It is important to surround ourselves with people who are willing to give up something in order to make life a little better for one another. It is fundamental to raising a family, building a team, supporting a town, or creating a diplomatic world. Sometimes there is a misunderstanding around that word. Some may see it as misfortune to give up or go without something. In actuality, sacrifice delights in the greater good. We are humbled to improve something meaningful in our lives or make improvements for the next generation. That lesson goes all the way back to the Bible, and it has been instrumental in my life. In fact, that principle led me to start playing around with a larger vision for myself. I started to test myself in larger settings by writing neighborhood newsletters, organizing a supper club, going to PTA meetings, and holding jewelry parties, make-up parties and block parties. Those were fun because it was a way to gather people together, but I wasn't exactly changing the world. Little did I know that someone was about to wake up a deeper part of my soul.

It's funny how our own sense of preparedness will often spark a new beginning or invite blessings into our lives. The Universe has a way of coming to our rescue, or anticipating our need by delivering opportunities and people into our lives at just the right time. It's those divine moments that we are elevated to another level of love. We may not recognize it, but that is grace, and it is happening all the time. The Universe has a way of nudging us in a different direction and responding to our subconscious energy. I am a firm believer in the Law of Attraction. There is a cause and effect to our energy. When we open our mind and prepare loving intentions then positive motion will happen. It is a little like tapping the Universe on the shoulder and saying, "I'm ready now."

In 1999 I found myself to be ready. I was celebrating my first Mother's Day. My sister, Sandy, surprised my mother, Gail, my other sister, Sylvia, and myself with tickets to a women's conference in San Francisco hosted by Willie Brown. Sandy and I were new mothers at the time. Our babies were only two weeks apart. We actually attended the conference wearing matching leather messenger bags. We looked sophisticated from a distance. One might have thought that we had laptops or important papers inside but upon further inspection, people could see that we were carrying our four hundred dollar Madela Double Breast Pumps. It was ridiculous and true. I mention that detail because most new mothers feel very vulnerable following birth. It's tough for new moms to get out of their pajamas and go to the market for groceries. New mamas are tired and emotional, and they are trying to establish some new routine that makes sense. Going to this conference may not have made great sense to some people, but I was sure that the Universe wanted me there. When we learned that Oprah Winfrey was the keynote speaker, we were determined to make it happen. She had hero status in our lives. She didn't know it, but she was my mentor. She had inspired me for years through her talk show and the Angel Network. In fact, she was the first person that introduced me to the word ***soul.***

Excitement poured out of me. I had been such a huge fan for so many years, and I knew that she would be amazing. I was so ready to hear something profound and meaningful. It didn't matter that I was emotionally stretched, that my boobs were engorged, or that I had not slept for more than a few hours. I was all in! I was there for a reason, and I wanted to hear something that would change my life. It's funny that I sat in an auditorium with a few thousand people, but I was sure that Oprah was talking just to me. To her credit, she has a way of getting right down to the core.

She had deep questions about life and service. She asked the audience, "What is your gift, and how will you use it for some greater good in the world?" I knew a few things about myself. I knew that I enjoyed gathering friends together, I loved rich conversations with women, and I liked to help people. I wasn't exactly sure how that passion would translate to service or a purpose in my life. I was just glad that I did not have to figure it all out in that moment. I could just listen, breathe, and receive.

I was riveted by Oprah's grace and her story of perseverance. She was living proof that greatness can come from the most humble beginnings, and we all have a destiny to fulfill. Looking back, I can now appreciate the best advice that she offered to us on that day. She told everyone to go home, make reflection a priority, and ask the Universe for a spiritual purpose. That was a powerful experience because I was challenged to go a little deeper than I had ever done before. That was the moment that Oprah opened the door to new possibilities. There was this little spark that started to flicker. I left that conference excited. I felt wide awake. I was lighter, more joyful, and aware of my own grace. It was as if a little wind came up underneath my wings. I didn't know it, but that little spark would eventually catch fire and become an inferno of love in my life and my community.

Has there been a divine moment in your life when you were steered in a new positive direction? How did that shift change your vision of yourself and the world? What is a special gift that you have identified in yourself? How can this translate to a higher calling in your life?

#GRACE

FULL CIRCLE MISSION

One of the reasons that I love the cover of this book is because it reinforces the message that most things in life come full circle. That doesn't mean that life is fair or that we will never experience pain or grief. The terms of our life are not always within our control, but we certainly have a choice in how we choose to respond to situations. We don't always realize it, but the Universe is quietly working in the background. It constantly lines up people, bestowing opportunities, and synchronizing moments. It has a way of shifting the wind and changing the course of our lives. Without any warning, we can find ourselves in the middle of a storm or a miracle, or in some cases, both.

When I left the Oprah conference, I was exhilarated and looking for a big change to happen. For some reason, I thought that I would go home and the Universe would immediately grace me with an amazing purpose. I also thought that it would reveal itself in some dramatic fashion. Although I was paying way more attention to my life and praying for some new *soul purpose*, nothing happened right away. The Universe had a much more methodical plan for me. Years passed, and I was able to put other priorities together. I was raising my new family, and starting a new sandwich business with Paul. Looking back, I now see how important it was to establish a strong foundation within my own life before I could ever commit to a larger calling in the world. Isn't it funny how things always seem to make a little more sense later? What I considered to be late was actually divine timing. I am learning that most blessings present themselves in our lives when we are emotionally and spiritually ready. It is true. When we open our mind to new ideas and our heart to new possibilities then the Universe can reveal what the next step is in our journey.

It wasn't until five years later when my sister and I called several compassionate women over to my house to help a friend in need that my spiritual calling revealed itself. A beautiful mother at my son's school, Carol, had a five year old and a newborn. She and her husband, Ron, had settled into a sweet life in Petaluma, California. Their immediate family lived outside the country. While they were visiting their family in England, Ron came down with a terrible staph infection. That infection quickly spread and claimed his life. Carol came back to Petaluma, and she found herself alone with two children. It was a terrible twist of fate. I wondered how something so unfair could happen to such nice people. I imagined what I would do in her situation, and I quickly realized that our community would have to step up in a way that only family would.

My sister, Sandy, and I rallied a bunch of friends, neighbors, and moms from school together. We didn't mind that some of the people did not know Carol because we understood that anyone could embrace her story and realize the need for compassion, empathy, and love. The gathering for Carol was pretty informal. I asked everyone to come casual, bring a plate of food or a beverage to share, and I encouraged people to bring a friend along. The intention for the evening was to show support and let Carol know that she was not alone. The night was powerful, and it had many layers to it. We shared stories, exchanged hugs, and the thirty women that came over settled into their purpose for the evening. We were all reminded of just how fragile life is and just how much it means to step up for others during difficult times. We quietly understood that hardships and tragedy can come on at any time, and we can never be too sure when it might be our turn.

During the evening I organized a talking circle. The collective energy in the room was warm and positive. We were able to listen to Carol tell her story. She expressed concern about what her life would look like after such a painful loss. In that fragile moment, our circle became a safe place for Carol to share her feelings and her fear about what life would be like moving forward. I can remember feeling so honored to hold her vulnerability, and there was this collective grace in the room. Every woman was touched to her core. Although Carol was at a low moment dealing with her grief, something else was being born—community kindness and philanthropy.

After we shared loving exchanges in the circle, I asked everyone in the room to think about helping Carol with a small financial donation. I put out a plain white paint can in the middle of the table and left it up to everyone to decide what they wanted to give. I reminded the group that their loving presence was an incredible gift, but a little help from everyone could help make Carol's life easier. I knew that any amount of money collected would be helpful, but I was not prepared for the generosity that happened. A small group of women quickly raised a thousand dollars. The paint can was filled with dollars, coins and personal checks. I cried when I realized the miracle that had occurred.

That money could not change what happened to Ron, but it restored some hope that night. Carol ultimately used that money to help her move back to England where she could be close to her family. I suppose that night not only sparked a new beginning for Carol, but it opened the door to a new charitable calling in my life.

That moment was nothing short of grace. I remember going to bed that night with a prayer of gratitude.
This is it. This is what I was searching for. Thank you for using me God. I will keep it going.

Has there been a moment in your life when everything seemed to line up beautifully by the Universe and your heart felt called to use your life for some greater purpose?

#GIVE

FLYING IN FABULOUS FORMATION

It is an incredible feeling to take flight. There is freedom and confidence when we find a passionate outlet into which to pour our love. As rewarding as it is to soar on our own, there is a special feeling when we join forces with others. We are stronger in a pack. There is a power and durability when we stand together, fight together and pray together. I love the image of geese and ducks flying in perfect V-formation. There is grace and beauty and depth and spirit. To peer up to clouds and see an awesome display of teamwork is nothing short of a miracle. Each bird takes their position and they fly in unison. They are careful and cooperative at all times. While there is a lead bird, they actually rotate the position. All of this is done with the intention to conserve fuel, brave the elements, and fulfill a mission. When humans collaborate for a charitable cause, we can observe that same grace and beauty. I think humanity is our version of flying in V-formation. There is indescribable feeling that happens when a community accepts a mission to fly together. It is human nature at its best.

The first gathering for Carol took place in 2005. My sister, Sandy, and I talked about that night extensively. We replayed all the love and magic that happened during the evening. We had some excitement about keeping the group going and supporting other meaningful causes. In fact, I started talking about the concept to anyone that would listen. I began holding gatherings every few months. It was the same simple format, bring an appetizer or beverage to share, support a brave cause or a family with an extraordinary hardship, and put out that magic paint can. The first few gatherings were held at my house.

It wasn't very long until people in the community began offering to host events in their own homes. We watched the attendance grow, and the community started suggesting families and meaningful causes. From the very start, I kept a scrapbook to recap the beautiful moments. I would send out an email to highlight what charitable cause we supported and report the amount of money raised. People started to love the positive exchange between themselves and the community. In fact, it was our local newspaper, *The Argus*, which wrote, "Those Fabulous Women are up to it again." It was then that the Universe decided to give us a name, and so we went with it. We were—*The Fabulous Women*!

Once the community started to recognize our group as a charitable force, we decided to formalize into a nonprofit charity. This was an important decision for our organization. We were able to expand our reach and establish a professional role in our community. The public understood that this wasn't an exclusive group. Although it was birthed by a small group of women in a living room, it was open to everyone. Pretty soon we had every facet of the community involved; men, women, business owners, public service officials, senior citizens, Boy Scout & Girl Scout Troops, and local schools. It became a grassroots movement to help worthy causes and come to the aid of families that had experienced life threatening illness, grief, or some unfortunate tragedy. I started to notice that I was not the only person who was longing for a purpose. In fact, we started witnessing some of the most poetic acts of love.

The Fabulous Women teamed up with the Petaluma American Little League (PALL) on a project called, Angel in the Outfield. It was a mission to reconstruct an old baseball field and pay tribute to a beautiful boy named, Trevor Smith. Trevor was called to heaven much too young. He had a vibrant smile and contagious energy. He made friends easily and although he was young, he understood life's most important values, faith, love, and family. Baseball was Trevor's favorite sport, and he loved spending time at the local field. When the community lost him, we struggled to find peace. It was clear that everyone wanted to hold onto his goodness. It became a natural decision to honor Trevor on the grounds that he loved so much. That is how the idea for the field project was born. It seemed fitting to restore the old dilapidated field to make a special dedication to his family.

Yes, that renovation became a sacred and healing mission for our community. It was a beautiful collaboration. The Fabulous Women rallied the community to raise money for the project and the little league coordinated the labor and the volunteers. Everyday people were taking extraordinary steps to show their support. Fred Hilliard was a board member on the PALL, and he was simply amazing on this project. He rallied the little league dads together, and they poured their love into the project. It took several months to complete their entire mission. They tilled the soil, laid the sod, painted the backstops and erected a beautiful monument. Fred paid attention to every single detail including the installation of a state of the art scoreboard that read Smith Field. Yes, it took many hands, but their sweat and hard work helped transform a neglected patch of grass into a sacred playing field.

There was something very wholesome and grassroots about that project. While our community understood that we couldn't bring Trevor back, we wanted to honor his extraordinary qualities and recognize that his young life had profound meaning. Trevor inspired people of all different ages to smile from deep within their soul. He was only in middle school, and yet his friendships stretched across the whole town. He enrolled in youth programs at school and church that highlighted leadership, service, and charity. He showcased his joyful spirit through a local theatre group, and he got involved with community sport teams. It was easy to see why the community embraced Trevor's story on such a profound level. In many ways that field allowed everyone to remember Trevor's goodness and uphold a positive role model for youth.

Smith Field will always hold a special place in my heart. It reminds me of Trevor's beautiful soul and the incredible love that poured through the community at a sad time. When I asked Fred about his role in the project he choked up and said, "It's hard to put into words the reward that I felt in taking the lead on this project. In some ways, I felt like I was chosen for this spiritual assignment. I thought about my own children and how life is very precious and unpredictable. I wondered why more people don't find ways to get involved with charity. You can never really explain what that feeling is like in your heart. You just have to be willing to put yourself way out there." People like Fred are all around us, waiting for an assignment. We must remember that charity is sometimes elusive. Yes, sometimes you will get an actual call from someone you know to come out and help. Other times we must pay attention to the whispers from the Universe and the spiritual nudges that come from within. The heart is our compass and it gravitates toward situations where love is abundant and other places where love is in short supply. It becomes our amazing choice to stretch ourselves, expand our role in the world, and explore meaningful ways to exchange love.

Yes, people all around me were connecting with our philanthropic ideas. I met a guy named Geoff Green. He had a smile the size of Texas. When he learned about the mission of our organization, he called our group and asked, "Do you need chicken? Because I got chicken!" He searched his heart and his resources, and that was what he had to give. Our group took Geoff up on his offer and we served his chicken at our nonprofit launch. I often think about Geoff and that beautiful offering. It made me think about the simplicity of charity. I saw it in a whole new way. I saw that this group gave people the chance to ask themselves what they could do to get involved. Whether it was a few hours of volunteering, baking brownies for a bake sale, installing a wheel chair ramp, digging out a field, or creating cookbooks for independent housing at the homeless shelter, I saw the most beautiful and fearless acts of love. No matter who it was, regardless of age, gender, or financial status, the gestures always seemed to come from the same beautiful place: the soul. It is where grace lives and miracles are born. Yes, the community exchanges were becoming larger and the Universe started trusting our group with the most sensitive stories from our town. Although Petaluma heritage had always rested its reputation on eggs and chicken farms, it was now embracing a new philanthropic identity.

As a community, we were adopting universal causes, The Boys & Girls Club and 4-H, and we were creating awareness about important issues: domestic violence, mentoring children, and homelessness, and we also championed a campaign for The National Bone Marrow Registry. We started raising awareness about silent diseases that touched members of our community, Multiple Sclerosis, Diabetes, Nevus, Cystic Fibrosis, and Cancer. We even took on a global project to help build a school in Rwanda. Yes, the Fabulous Women were really soaring and I could not contain my excitement.

The birth of this group reaffirmed that there is strength in numbers, and we should do everything humanly possible to help divide pain and multiply love. I know that alone I can be helpful, but the real magic happens when people from all walks of life come together to make sacrifices for the greater good. That original group of women that once came over to my house to support Carol had experienced a moment of grace. I was later impressed to witness that happen on a much more significant level. Over the years our group has orchestrated special events that have gathered a few thousand people together. It is amazing what happens when people show up for all the right reasons. Blessings come to the surface and the heart of a town is revealed. People quickly learn that they may have showed up to be helpful to someone in need, but they are the ones that walk away feeling blessed.

I have thought a lot about the power of the collective spirit. Call it what you will, humanity, community, family, neighborhood, team, sisterhood, brotherhood, church, book club or an Orange Army. There is simply no denying the power and grace that happens when people come together in the name of service and love. It's a little like poetry. There is something brilliant about meal trains and putting a casserole on a porch for someone who has been sick. It is awesome to see school children run a lemonade stand for a family in need. It is harmonious to witness a high school football team wear orange cancer ribbons on their helmets and dedicate their season to their hero with Leukemia. It broadcasts a message to those who are suffering: **We are in this**

together. Yes, it is indescribable to watch humanity unfold and see how little simple gestures can help heal the human spirit and validate someone at their darkest hour. After all, life and vulnerability are often simultaneous. We take turns being strong and broken. Every day we are challenged to show up for others around us, and it's up to us to respond to the call. I think there is great pride in knowing that we belong to an extended family that anchors to compassion. As a country we felt it after 9/11. As a community I felt it when our town has rallied around CJ Banaszek during his leukemia battle. I have come to the realization that when we put all of the tiny acts of kindness together, hope happens. It creates solidarity and a force field of love.

If we choose to become strengthened, more focused and directed with a purpose, our pain is without vain. Human kindness and life lessons may in fact be the silver lining in the worst moments imaginable. I saw this firsthand early in our organization when we dealt with a harrowing loss of a child. I had a lovely friend named Ling Murray. She and I played volleyball together on Wednesday nights. She had a two year old daughter named Calli who loved to run around the gym during scrimmages. On a beautiful day that looked like any other day, Ling brought Calli to the park. As they were walking home they were struck by a vehicle in the crosswalk. The young driver was texting at the time. Ling and her husband, Jeff, lost their sweet two year old daughter. Ling also suffered critical physical injuries. I can remember thinking that nothing good could come from this tragedy; nothing good at all.

Because our group had a friendship with the Murray Family, it was an easy decision to help them raise money for Ling's hospital bills. As a philanthropic group we had established a reputation for helping families with extraordinary hardship, but this unfortunate tragedy felt very personal. We knew that we could not change Calli's destiny, but we were bound and determined to find the silver lining and raise faith and hope in the hearts of the community. Literally hundreds and hundreds of people showed up to our fundraiser for Ling and her husband, Jeff. The owners of a local venue, Sally Tomatoes, opened the doors to host the event. Businesses donated generous raffle baskets and auction items, people baked goods to sell, families brought food to share, Girl Scout troops ran the bake sale, local news channels covered the story, and a popular band, Wonder Bread 5, donated live music to draw in the public. It seemed like every facet of the community got involved. Local law enforcement and the fire department personnel showed up to pay their respects and promote a message of safety. I was particularly touched by my friend, Ani Larson. She was also on our volleyball team. She organized a band of youth to show up to help volunteer for the day. As a sixth grade teacher she had always promoted the mantra, *It's Nice to be Nice*. Those kids were excellent contributors for the day. They helped with raffle sales, food distribution, and clean-up. I suppose I'm raising awareness to all these details because it felt like our entire community came together for the Murray Family.

It reaffirmed that charity has no age restriction, and it is important to teach compassion early. Yes, it was an amazing display of love and it was gratifying to see the community embrace this family at such a difficult time. I have to say that I found myself trying to put into words all the tangled emotions that were in the room that day. I found myself speechless. The truth was something tragic and beautiful was happening at the same time. It was a new experience that left me feeling humbled.

On that day everyone was asked to take a pledge against distracted driving. Purple thumb bands were given to every single guest to remind them to put the phone down when operating a vehicle. I think it was one of the most important lessons that we were supposed to learn from Calli's story. Yes, we were all humbled by the Universe, and we knew that this twist of fate was supposed to serve some greater good. The exchange of Calli's life did not seem fair, but there was some higher purpose that was unfolding. We all knew that safety and compassion were the take away lessons. While we had not fully digested the experience, that community fundraiser helped clarify our priorities. Calli's life would remind the world that there isn't a single message on our phone that cannot wait until later. Distracted driving is all too common, and we are forever called to pay attention to the road and pay attention to our lives.

I am convinced that this formula for charity works because of its simplicity. Every person big or small can participate. It assembles itself on easy components, sharing time with people, enjoying stimulating conversations, eating good food, listening to brave stories, exchanging wisdom, creating new friendships, and helping someone at a time of great need. It resonates with everyone. I have had time to compile ten years of gathering and giving. I now know that the finest reward of this group has been the gentle unfolding of our own hearts. I am quite convinced that life and charity are circular. In giving love to others, we also become the recipients of kindness. I also know that Petaluma Spirit exists worldwide, and every town has the power to create its own charitable movement. It just takes a few courageous people to lead the way.

When I began writing *Soul Purpose* I felt so strongly about telling the story about the birth of our organization and how we formalized into a nonprofit. The Fabulous Women of Sonoma County has been a blessing, and it is another reason that *Soul Purpose* came to be. I am filled with gratitude. I have realized that so much of my experience and knowledge has come from the brave families that have shared their stories with our group. I have always felt that it was an honor to hold their stories and their pain even if it was for just a brief moment. What I quickly came to realize is that their energy doesn't leave. It rests in the heart of our organization. Their families have become the thread and the fabric that keeps our organization strong. In some greater way, the courage of those families has helped us become better human beings. Their love and their stories carry on. I had hoped that this book would convey my gratitude to them. I want every family that has moved through the arms of this group to know that something significant happened when they trusted us and shared their stories with the community. They taught us powerful lessons of love. They reminded us to be compassionate, unselfish and grateful, and while none of that seems like a fair exchange for their pain. This book is a declaration of love to them.

Have you ever experienced a moment of grace when a group came together for a profound purpose or charitable cause? What was the feeling that you experienced? Is there something in your life that allows you to get involved with your community to make a positive contribution?

#COMMUNITY

For more information on how to start a similar group in your community, email us: TheFabulousWomen@gmail.com.

SOARING TO NEW HEIGHTS

I love to tell the story about how The Fabulous Women got started because it was a profound moment in my life, and I can look back and see the ripples of love in our community. At a glance, it may have seemed like I stumbled onto a purpose, but the truth is that I was inviting passion and service into my life for a very long time. It removes the notion that things are coincidental. Instead, it validates just how powerful we are when we team up with the Universe.

When we invite change and positive goals into our lives, doors start to open, and opportunities present themselves. It speaks to the law of attraction. We are amazing human beings with powerful thoughts and suggestions. We can always choose to turn up the volume of love in our lives and amplify positive energy. We can also broadcast negativity. It is entirely our choice, and either decision will impact the tone of our relationships and our experience. We were never created to live in fear, sadness, and depression. Our worth is determined by our belief in ourselves and our faith in something bigger than ourselves. We aren't always aware of it, but the Universe is listening to us, and it will respond to our intentions. We each have the power to manifest our dreams and turn our plans into a reality. That's wonderful news for people seeking, searching, praying, exploring and placing positive intentions in the world. Yes, I'm talking to all of you that believe that the glass is half full and that everything is serving a higher purpose.

Synchronicity is defined in the Merriam Webster Dictionary as, *"the coincidental occurrence of events and especially psychic events (as similar thoughts in widely separated persons or a mental image of an unexpected event before it happens) that seem related but are not explained by conventional mechanisms of causality."*

Whether we realize it or not, synchronicity is happening all the time. It can be something as simple as willing the perfect parking space in the rain, or it can be something much more profound. I can seriously look back at my life and note countless episodes of synchronicity.

In the beginning, I wasn't sure what to call it. I thought they were just lucky moments. I was just in the right place at the right time. We have all heard of the term coincidence. Yes, that's just another cool word that also means synchronicity. It's when the Universe hands us some fortunate moment to affirm our path and our positive energy. It can be a person that shows up in our lives at just right the time, an opportunity that falls in our lap, or some karmic reward that feels a little like grace. Some of my literary friends like to call these little miracles 'Invisible Threads.'

I have had several moments that felt like my Higher Power was orchestrating blessings. They always seem to happen when I am making a request to serve, love, or express gratitude. I can remember a great little story that highlights the collaborative energy that occurred between myself and the Universe. Our nonprofit was given five ten pound blocks of cheese for a fundraiser. It was a little embarrassing that we only used about 20 slices. I asked our board what we would do with all that cheese. I certainly didn't want it to go to waste, and I wanted to honor the goodness in which it was donated. It sounds crazy, but I prayed that we would find a home for that cheese. The next day, I received sad news that a friend in the community had passed away. I later got a call from the person organizing the memorial wondering if I knew someone who could donate cheese. I bit my tongue because I couldn't get the words out fast enough, "I have the cheese! Oh my goodness, I have the cheese!"

Another moment of grace that comes to mind is when my sixteen year old son, Frank, got very sick from a staph infection resulting from a turf burn while he was at a football camp. He became so ill it compromised his immune system and disrupted his stomach function. He eventually became septic and he was admitted to the hospital. It was a scary time for my family. We could not figure out how our boy who was in the best physical shape of his life could become so weak and feeble. Over the course of six months doctors struggled to diagnose Frank's stomach condition. Frank became sidelined from life. He was unable to eat regular meals, he missed a lot of school, and he could not play sports. I can remember staying at the hospital with him for a week. At night I would quietly pray, "God, I'm not sure why my boy has to go through all of this, but whatever the reason, use me for some service. This needs to turn into something good." It took a very long time, but Frank was eventually diagnosed. Because of all the different infections in his body and all of the harsh antibiotics, he had a serious gastrointestinal issue. We could not have diagnosed him, if we did not have technology.

Now, here is the synchronicity part of the story. A month after Frank's health was restored I got a call from the local hospital foundation notifying me that I was chosen for a leadership award in my town. They wanted to acknowledge the positive impact that our group was having on the charitable spirit of the community. They asked if I would prepare a speech about charity and help them raise money for their cause for the evening. I felt honored and asked what they were raising money for. They asked me to imagine how scary it would be to have a loved one in the hospital with serious gastrointestinal problems that could not be properly diagnosed.

They said their focus for the event was to raise money to purchase state of the art, high definition gastroenterology equipment. I said, "Are you kidding me? That is how I spent the last six months of my life with my son!" I questioned whether they had prior knowledge about my son's health, and they were emphatic that it was a coincidence. Because Frank was treated at another hospital in a different area I had to believe that my prayers in the hospital were heard, and something that posed the worst fear and the biggest hardship in our lives was now going to be used for some greater good. It was pure hell worrying about my boy, and it was pure torture to find out that he had become septic and his life was in jeopardy. Strangely, something miraculous came from all it. Frank's story was shared at the hospital benefit. He indirectly helped raise medical awareness, improve patient care, and advance the technology in our local hospital. Now that was an incredible twist of fate and grace!

I have just one more story about synchronicity that I have to share with you. It is my absolute favorite! In 2010 I was invited to my friend, Debbie Abram's house. She was a local radio deejay host, so she's met some pretty cool people. She called me and says, "Hey, I want you to come meet my amazing friend, Marla. She's a pet psychic and she does Reiki." I was happy to go. It sounded like a fun night. Well, Debbie was right about Marla. She was pretty amazing! Everyone spent one on one time with her. I found myself very receptive to her bodywork and riveted by her psychic readings. Interestingly, Marla had some homemade homeopathic sprays that she was selling. I said that I was interested in her Opportunity Spray. She proceeded to ask me what I wanted in my life. I then told her about the gift of The Fabulous Women, and how Oprah inspired me to create a charitable mission in our community. I told her that I wanted to go to Chicago to meet Oprah on the final season of her talk show and thank her for the life changing inspiration to start this charity group. Without hesitation, Marla hands me the bottle and tells me to take home the spray and use it daily. She told me to spray it on myself and offer the intention to the Universe to go to The Oprah Show. I was a willing spirit, so I bought the spray for $19.99. That night I committed to the ritual. In fact, I took it even further, and I changed my password on my email to Oprah 16. I knew that I would be logging onto my computer several times a day, and I knew that 16 was my lucky number. I thought it wouldn't hurt to leverage my intentions and really try to convince the Universe that I was determined to meet Oprah.

A month passed and Oprah's website posed the question, "Why are you Oprah's Ultimate Fan?" Well, I wrote a few short paragraphs about the birth of our organization and talked about Oprah's inspiration in my life. I expressed my gratitude for Oprah and shared my passion for charity. I hit send and didn't really give it another thought. A few weeks later I received an email message from Harpo Studios. It informed me that I had been chosen to be a guest of the Oprah Winfrey Show. The message said that I could bring a guest and needed to respond within twenty four hours. My heart jumped out of my chest. I was elated. It happened—and it happened to me! Tears rushed down my face. I was going to see Oprah Winfrey! I also could not believe that it landed on the sixteenth day of November! It didn't matter that I didn't know the topic of her show. In my mind she chose me, and I was blessed a hundred times over. Because my sister, Sandy, was the first person to take me to the Oprah Conference five years earlier and she helped me start The Fabulous Women, I chose her to go on the adventure. That moment was incredible! I felt like I was in some crazy fairy tale. Things were coming full circle, and I was absolutely sure that the Universe had everything to do with it.

The closer we got to November 16th the more difficult it became to contain my enthusiasm. It was an unbelievable opportunity. The only information that I knew about the show was that I was invited because somewhere in Oprah's career, she had inspired me to start a movement of kindness. This was incredible validation. It was based on my heart and service. I wasn't wealthy, fashionable, or famous. I was not a good singer, I didn't act, and I wasn't an Olympic athlete. I was just me. I liked to give. I liked to help people and inspire others to be charitable too. Somehow, that moment reaffirmed a simple fact. We are bound together by love. It is our hearts that connect us on the most universal level. It is not stature, wealth, or prestige. In fact, I'm reminded of a wonderful Italian proverb that my mother-in-law loves, "At the end of the game the pawn and the king go back in the same box."

The trip to Chicago was like a dream. That moment made me believe that miracles can happen at any time to anyone. We reported to Harpo Studios at 7:30 in the morning, lined up with others and started making small talk. No one else had a clue why they were invited to the show either. Those conversations turned out to be an amazing part of my experience. Every person that I talked to had created some beautiful mission to serve or improve the world. One person was collecting backpacks for inner city kids, another person was doing work in Africa, and there were medical rescue people there who had saved lives. I felt so honored to be among the heroes and philanthropists.

We were all ushered into her studio, and we nervously waited to hear what the show was all about. My sister and I were giddy and nervous. A producer stepped out into the crowd and said, "Congratulations, you have been chosen for the Hometown Hero Show! In a moment you will have the opportunity talk about your charitable project and tell Oprah how she has inspired your mission." We were beside ourselves. I thought, *are you kidding me*? We get to go on stage and talk about charity with Oprah! The whole thing felt unbelievable and my heart was revving like a NASCAR. I'm not sure that I had fully completed a single thought when Oprah stepped into the studio. She was dressed in a simple black dress and she seemed a bit serious. I can remember holding my heart as the intensity in the room grew stronger and stronger. She then took a nice long deep breath and pleasantly looked around the studio. She humorously nudged the crowd, "Ya'll must be exhausted from all that giving!" The crowd laughed, and she proceeded with a question, "I'm wondering just how many of you take time to replenish yourselves with quiet meditation?" A chime that you would hear in a Buddhist temple rang, and the crowd got slightly uncomfortable. We were not sure where Oprah's conversation was going next. To be honest, I had watched Oprah for most of my life, and I have to say that it was a very strange beginning to a show. Oprah said that she suspected that most of us found it difficult to relax and replenish. Given the fact that only a few people raised their hands, Oprah instructed everyone to settle in, take a deep breath, and take a moment to meditate. With that, the sound of jingle bells rang through the studio, the stage opened up to the most incredible winter wonderland scene that you have ever seen, snow came fluttering down into her studio and landed on our faces, and Oprah slipped her arms out of that drab little dress. Underneath was the most beautiful red Christmas gown that I've ever seen. Pardon my curse, but I looked at my sister and said, "Oh shit, we're on Oprah's 'Favorite Things' show!" I could not believe what I was seeing. There were elves pouring down the runway, purses rolling on conveyer belts, and the stage lit up with thousands of sparkling Christmas lights.

I couldn't catch my breath. How does this happen? The moment was too big to fit in my head. This was the same giveaway show that I watched every season in my living room. I always loved seeing the faces of people who were surprised by Oprah, and now I was that crazy woman screaming, crying and jumping up and down. Oprah eventually got the room quiet and said the kindest most genuine words, "If somewhere in my twenty-five year career I was able to inspire you to use your life for a path of service, then I am the grateful one. That is why you are here and that is my gift to you. Thank you." Tears were streaming down my cheeks. It was so ironic. I wanted so desperately to get to Chicago to offer some prayer of thanks to Oprah for taking me to another level in my life, and just like that, she turned the table. It was her incredible reward to see that her life had purpose and some legacy of love and service.

People often ask me about the stuff that I got on that show. I suppose I would ask someone the same question, but my response is never quite as exciting as people want to hear. My answer has always remained the same, "The stuff was cool, but it was never about the stuff." It was the full circle moment that brought me the greatest joy. It was the reward of seeing the seeds that Oprah planted fifteen years earlier grow in my life, it was the validation of the birth of an amazing movement called The Fabulous Women, and it was the incredible epilogue that happened on that chilly November day in Chicago when I stood face to face with my mentor and my idol. To me, that was the best stuff!

If you took a moment out of your day to reflect back on your own life, I bet you would find several examples of grace and synchronicity. It's not about being lucky. Miracles become a little easier to identify when we are paying attention to love and practicing gratitude. There were many years in my life where I wandered the planet oblivious to my energy. As far as I was concerned, life was happening to me. I had no say in it. I had no intentions, and I didn't set any real attainable goals. The idea of manifesting dreams and paving love into my day seemed kind of silly. Once I bought into my own worth and my spiritual power, I could shift my energy toward positive experiences and meaningful exchanges. I have also realized that most of the things that unfold in our favor don't always start out that way. This was the case with my son's illness and the leftover cheese. I can now see that I was using my energy to co-create a positive outcome. I do realize that things don't always work out just because we say intentions out loud, but I'm convinced that our positive attitudes and our participation will afford us many amazing opportunities and blessings.

Our participation and our attitude is a key component to our health and happiness. If we can remember that every day we have the opportunity to use our lives for something positive, then the Universe will figure out the rest. It's like anything else in our lives. It becomes a spiritual practice to welcome love and blessings into our lives. In fact, it isn't until we honor the grace that already lives inside of us that it starts to make a regular appearance in our lives. If that sounds like a foreign idea, I can sum it up very simply. When you wake up in the morning, establish a simply routine. Say two things out loud: *Thank you* and *use me for some greater good today*. This will allow a quiet space for goodness to flow into our hearts, into our homes, and into the world.

Can you site a moment in your life where synchronicity happened? Are there positive intentions that you can create for your daily practice that will take your dreams and heart to another level of love and joy?

#DIVINITY

LEAVE THE KEY UNDER THE MAT

I have come to love the saying *Gather on Purpose*. For me, it is represents the gift of coming together with people for positive reasons. It is an inspiring anthem for charity. I have found that charity works at its very best when we make a personal decision to get involved and we honor powerful intentions to do good deeds in the world. Whether it's helping a sick friend, joining a relief movement, or carrying out an act of kindness, we declare in our hearts that something outside of ourselves is important and worthy of our time and sacrifice. It's a way to create deeper connections in our lives, and discover larger reasons for living. Charity is not a *have to*. It's a *get to*. There will be some people in this world that will never experience the reward or goodness of giving. It is not because they don't have the heart strings or the capacity for love. We are all inherently good. We are all born with a beating heart and a hungry soul. It's because they have not declared its importance. Some people will talk themselves out of charity by saying they have no money or no time. *Soul Purpose* challenges the world to utilize our most personal and precious gift that we all have, LOVE.

After many years of gathering the community for charity, I have come to realize that there are a few simple questions that we can all ask ourselves to determine our charitable priorities. What do you want to be remembered for? Will it be the fearless acts of love that have flowed through your relationships and your community? Does your current energy mirror the love in your heart and the passion in your soul? Those are questions that we all must figure out for ourselves.

One of the greatest individuals that I have ever had the privilege of knowing was James Forni. He was a teacher, a basketball coach, and an amazing leader in our community. He was an idol for so many young people in our community, including my son, Frank. He was battle tested by cancer. For years he held an inspirational mantra to help him stay focused during his journey with melanoma. It was *Vincero*, an Italian phrase that means, *I will win*. For James, it meant living to his potential, expressing love in the most profound ways, and facing his fears.

James Forni was an exceptional human being, and he was victorious on every level of his life because he was courageous and he continuously performed simple acts of kindness. Every single day he conducted himself with the highest level of poise, grace, and charity. He was so passionate about teaching and coaching. It gave him the platform to do what he loved most—be with people, mentor them through challenges, and share stories and laughter. James understood that rich and meaningful exchanges were happening every moment. He held court in the locker room and on the sidelines during a timeout. He understood that some of the greatest conversations with kids were going to happen on his way to his car to go home. A parking lot discussion about perseverance and courage would occur almost daily. He was so humbled and unselfish with his time. His wife, Mary, would often joke and say that it was not uncommon for James to get home an hour late, but neither of them seemed to mind one bit. Talking with people was never an inconvenience or imposition. It was the time that

James relished and shined. Students looked up to him, players adored him, and his own peers and colleagues revered him with great respect. Yes, to know him was to love him. James made every person he interacted with feel like they were the most important person in the world.

James taught me and the rest of our community that quality human interaction remains the highest level charity that we can bring to our daily lives. Yes, charity may in fact be a lot simpler than most people think. It doesn't necessarily mean organizing a bake sale, raising money for a relief effort, or promoting world peace. It may be as simple as talking and listening to another human being, offering a hug to someone that is having a hard day, or just sitting with someone that feels sick or broken. We all have that beautiful potential. It remains a mystery why some people seem to carry out that grace so much easier than others. I can only arrive at the conclusion that people like James become spiritual teachers because they believe in something greater than themselves. James was a faith keeper. Grace always channeled through his interactions. He had a rhythm to his conversations. He was gentle and funny, and he was unselfish with his heart. That is why James Forni will always remain a tremendous spirit in our community. He was a champion in every manner of his life. He left it all out on the court, and we were blessed to witness his journey.

As we expand our definition of charity, I also hope *Soul Purpose* inspires more love and compassion in the world. When I was asked to prepare a speech for the hospital foundation in our community about charity, I sat down and wrote a piece I named The Secret Key. It is about the beautiful exchange that happens when we give away some part of our hearts. We must remember that giving something back to the world will create more ripples of love than we can ever measure. In fact, the greatest gift happens right inside our own soul.

The truth is when we elevate love in our lives and look for opportunities to serve others we begin to soar to new heights. Mother Teresa offered us one of the greatest quotes to reflect on while we are in pursuit of our greatness when she said, "It's not how much we give, but how much love we put into giving." Perhaps the best lesson that we can learn in this lifetime is that we already have everything we need to live, love and give. *Soul Purpose* is the awareness that our greatest gifts are already within us, and it becomes our calling to seize every moment possible to express them in the world.

The Secret Key

In our lives we will be graced with a few special keys. The first is the key to our home. This is where we raise our families, have heart to heart talks, and pray at the dinner table. It is the place that we tuck our children into bed and plant tulip bulbs in the spring; we celebrate holidays and milestones, grandpa's birthday, and a driver's permit. It is where we can be ourselves, celebrate our truth, and talk about dreams for the future. Yes, this key opens the door to our sacred space where we can laugh, cry, rest, and love.

The second key on our ring is to our car. It signifies our independence in the world. We come and go on brave adventures. We take ourselves to work, our kids to school, and our families to church. We work hard to balance it all. This key represents our journey and the courageous movement in our lives. The places we go and the people we meet become a part of our story. This is the key that reminds us that we are meant to continuously explore our hearts and find our larger purpose in the world.

There is a third key that I like to refer to as The Secret Key. This key opens the door to human kindness and philanthropy. Not everyone will use this key, only a few. These are the people with a charitable vision to improve the world. They use their imagination, their wisdom, and their positive energy to rally the troops. They understand how the collective spirit can inspire change, ignite passion and spread hope. Let this key remind you of your own heroic place in the world. Thank you for understanding that giving something back to your community is as much for your own fulfillment as it is for the next generation. What does it mean to be a leader? It means using that secret key often, and remembering that we are all in this together. It's living thoughtfully, and realizing your strength and personal responsibility. Because a good leader also understands that someone always forgets their key, and occasionally you'll have to put yours under the mat.

Allow yourself to invite the Vincero Spirit into your life. Where do you see a greater opportunity to practice charity in your daily exchanges?

#VINCERO

THE FLIGHT OF GRATITUDE

Well, here we are at the final chapter of this journey, and I am faced with the challenging task of wrapping things up and saying goodbye. Now, that has always been a little tricky in my life. I used to get upset when people moved on. To be perfectly honest, there have been many times in my life when I have tried to hold onto things too tight and for too long. Our lives will teach us over and over to adjust, shift, release, relinquish, adapt, let go, and move on. It does not matter if we are emotionally ready for it or not. It is just a part of life. The truth is that everything will run its course, and we will have to go through some painful goodbyes. Those experiences change who we are and they become important chapters in our story. Somehow, we have to trust that time heals the heart, and gratitude will find its way.

I have thought about some of the those tough goodbyes in my own life—graduations, career changes, moving away, friendships that have drifted apart, the passing of a parent, and seeing loved ones lose their battle with illness. It is hard to put into words. We cannot fully prepare for loss before it happens. It is much more complicated because we need to go through a grieving process. It's true, it can feel like you are barely hanging on when you are going through it. It raises big questions about what life will look like afterwards. On some level, we all know that grief is an individual experience and there is no right or wrong way to go through it. It is a passage that we walk through in our own time. We may not realize it, but we create the terms of a situation as soon as we invest heart into a person or an experience. It's a gift to form relationships that validate our soul and shape our identity, but when that connection is broken, we will also have to come to terms with the sadness and the changes.

We have witnessed some of the most heart wrenching losses and have experienced some very painful goodbyes. Our organization has centered its mission on supporting families that have experienced extraordinary hardships, so we have held families during their darkest hour. Although there are no words for their pain, there is one thing that has prevailed in those moments, LOVE. If we can remember that somewhere between our pain and our peace there is an unwavering space for love, then we can begin to heal. That means that we honor ourselves enough to allow our feelings and special memories to come to the surface. We care enough about ourselves to allow the goodness to emerge and lessons to unfold. We value ourselves enough to let people show up for us, offer their support and participate in our grief. Most importantly, we love ourselves enough to see the blessings beneath our tears. When we find the courage to say thank you to the Universe for allowing an experience or a person to come into our lives and touch the most sacred place in our heart, then we may step into our true grace.

We must remember that the reason why it hurts so much is because we have loved so deeply. It is a beautiful and tangled dynamic that raises the complexity of our lives, but if you ask anyone, they will tell you time and time again that it is all worth it. I suppose that is why I now believe that there is honor and privilege in goodbyes. If we take a moment at our time of sorrow and reflect on how that person or experience taught us to become better human beings, then we have truly embraced their goodness, and they carry on. My prayers and my soul searching have always led me to the same conclusion. Perhaps we were never really meant to say goodbye. Instead, we are just called to say thank you. Thank you for letting me hold you in my life for just a little while. Thank you for allowing me to expand my capacity for love and joy. Thank you for teaching me something beautiful about myself and the world. Yes, thank you!

Gratitude creates space for peace. It is true that we do not always have the say when people will leave us or when something will end, but we do have a choice in how we let it affect our lives. Sometimes saying goodbye may create space for something new to enter our lives, and what feels like an ending could also signify some new beginning. I can remember when my youngest son, Vince, graduated from elementary school. I got misty-eyed when I realized that both kids were all finished with the school. I had gotten attached to amazing teachers and the daily ritual of bag lunches and carpool. I thought to myself, "They're all done and so am I. I'm not ready!" I had this lump in my throat. I wasn't prepared for the emotions that I felt when I said goodbye to the crossing guard. I thought to myself, "For eleven years this person greeted me in the morning and provided safety to my children, and now I'm not going to see him anymore." Now that's a pretty simple example of how people affect us without realizing it. I am sure that we can site much deeper relationships that have really impacted our lives, teachers, childhood friends, first loves, college friends, neighbors, co-workers; the list goes on and on.

There is an old adage that my mom shared with me years ago. She found it in the back of the church bulletin. It read, "People will come into your life for a reason, a season, or a lifetime." That simple wisdom changed how I view the world and it changed how I view goodbyes. It helped me understand the law of nature and the beauty of purpose. It is the gentle reminder that every person we come in contact with has the potential to change our lives. If we choose to, we can create some loving impact or lasting impression on just about everyone. It doesn't always have to be a life-long situation. It could be a quick exchange at the market, a few semesters at school, a couple of years at a job, or some little chunk of time in our lives.

It is comforting to know that saying goodbye or parting ways does not always mean that anything is wrong. It may in fact mean that we have gone as far as we can go together, a lesson has been learned, an experience has been shared, and something new will grow in its place. That is my hope for this book, *Soul Purpose*. My prayer is that some part of your heart has cracked wide open and you see this moment as new beginning for yourself. *Soul Purpose* has never been about endings. It could only scratch the surface of our hearts and start a conversation about love, charity, and your beautiful purpose for living. From the front cover of this book all the way to the final page, I have wanted to bring a message of hope, celebration, and peace to the world. We must realize that we all have some larger stake in the world's progress and evolution. Believe it when I say that it all begins within our own personal journey to grow, spread love, and serve a larger calling outside of ourselves. That is really the best place to begin and insert our kindness.

It is true that in the greater scope of the universe we may be a tiny speck, but our roots are endless in length and one person can reach across the earth with the right message. I am in awe of what can happen when we bring good intentions to our lives. It all starts in our homes and carries over into our schools and our communities. From there anything is possible. How amazing to realize that we can have a hand in grooming a new generation that is responsible, kind, and compassionate. *Soul Purpose* depends on love and relies on all of us to pass on the best part of ourselves. For that reason, I could see no other way to finish this book than to compose a letter of love to my two sons, Frank and Vince. You don't have to be a parent to understand the message. What *Soul Purpose* has helped me realize is that our deepest intentions are pure, they hold universal love for the entire human race, and they are meant to be carried out in a way that is compassionate, joyful and sincere. That is the grace in which we were born and that is the gift that we hold every single day. In the end, we were always a part of something vast and beautiful, and we were meant to give something back. For that reason, it becomes our amazing honor to follow our passion, declare our Soul Purpose and take flight in our lives.

Be Brave
Be Faithful
Soar On ~

TO MY SONS

Dear Frank and Vince,

Let me begin with I love you. If you can remember that everything that truly matters begins and ends with love, then you will have rich and fulfilling lives. I could not ask for two better people to call my sons. Something amazing happened when you were born. From the very moment that you took your first breath in the world, I decided that I wanted to be a better person, and I wanted to find some way to make this world a better place for you to grow, play, and follow your heart. This book reflects a calling in my life to be voice of love and service. It is also a recording of life lessons that have gently floated to the top. I don't expect to save you from mistakes or hardship, but maybe some of my wisdom will rub off on you and somehow make your life easier. When I was pregnant I can remember asking God to hold a sacred space for you to have a joyful life. However, I now realize that it's completely up to you to figure out what your gifts are, realize your own special purpose, and decide what makes you happy. Nobody can do that for you. Your father and I will clear a path for you, and it will be our great pleasure to watch you become responsible and caring adults in the world.

When you are a parent, you quickly realize that your happiness is often tied to your children. It's difficult to see where our hearts end and where your stories begin. Despite my greatest intentions, I had to immediately come to terms with a few things. I wanted to be your rock, but sometimes I felt a bit unstable, I wanted to teach you about the world, but I didn't have all the answers, I wanted to be your friend but I would have to make unpopular decisions. Yes, parenthood sets the stage for the most ambitious love, and we are filled with the biggest fears and crazy doubts. Will I be a good parent? Am I enough? I didn't realize that my heart could skip a beat when you were sad, sick, or scared. I also didn't know that every hard lesson that I had to learn earlier in my life might just serve some greater purpose in your lives too. Yes, all that gentle wisdom would eventually become a daily glass of milk for my soul and I could feel grateful about passing it on to the two of you.

So, let's talk about all the fun that I want you to have. I hope you find the courage to try new things and take on bold adventures. Yes, during this lifetime, I hope you get a chance to dip your toes in Lake Tahoe, sing karaoke, see at least one Broadway show, and travel to some exciting places to hike, try new food, and experience culture. I've figured out that most things won't come to you. You'll have to be the one to seize the beauty and the opportunities all around you. Don't worry about whether you're good at it or not. Just look for amazing ways to grow and stretch your comfort zone. Oh yes, while I'm at it, you should plant at least one live tree in your life. I'm not talking about calling the gardener. I mean you take home that fragile little seedling pack, scout out the perfect location in the yard, and run your fingers through the soil. There's a lot to be learned by taking time in nature. It's soothing and peaceful to the soul. There's simply nothing sweeter than curling up next to a tree, listening to birds or the sound of a babbling brook, and getting quiet enough to hear the sound of your heartbeat.

TO MY SONS

I hope you understand the difference between material happiness and inner joy. Sometimes the world confuses the two, and I always want you to be clear on what you should fight for. Fight for people, fight for the truth, and fight for causes that raise hope and spread positive messages in the world. There is simply no material item that can replace human kindness. Sometimes you'll need a hug, and sometimes you'll have to give one. Keep your priorities clear and remember that loving exchanges are waiting for you at all times. If there is one thing that remains perfectly clear about the human spirit, we can all thrive under pressure, during adversity, and through sickness and grief if we keep love as our highest priority.

Frank and Vince, you were fortunate to understand the Warrior Spirit associated with **CJ Strong** and **Vincero.** I feel that the two of you were blessed to know and love CJ Banaszek and James Forni. Cancer may have taken them both too early, but it could never take away their dignity, their strength, and amazing life purpose. While they were tough losses in your lives, they graced you with the most important life lessons, perseverance, courage, and genuine love. Allow their spirit to drive you to another level of greatness in your life. That is a wonderful way to honor them and show your admiration.

I can remember when I was a young mother. Someone bought me the book *Love You Forever* by Robert Munsch. It's the perfect story about a mother's love for her son. I read it to the both of you over and over when you were little boys. I hope you get the chance to read it again as an adult. You'll understand the depth of my love, and you'll see that everything comes full circle. Yes, from a very young age I wanted to teach you about the importance of family. A lot of people will come in go in your lives. Family will be that constant force that celebrates milestones, helps you get through bumpy moments, and gives you a heritage to be proud of.

I love that you both got to know your four grandparents. I hope you look back fondly on your time together and realize that your grandparents always wanted the very best for you. Each one had something special to teach you. Papa Dan taught you to cheer on the local sports teams, bring poise to your life, and always plan for the future. Grandma Cathy taught you to live joyfully. She showed you that you can make friends just about anywhere, and she taught us that no holiday is complete without the stuffed eggs and the green Jell-O® mold. Grandma Gail taught you to grab hold of your faith. She wanted you to realize the small treasures in life, a family feast, time in the garden, or a game of Scrabble. Papa Mando, well, he taught you to be true to yourself, be a trail blazer, and have a sense of humor along the way. It's true. He was a man of few words. Every time he left you he said, *"Be good."* Those two words meant everything. It meant, "I love you, be safe, be true to your word, be fearless, be a leader, and follow your true north." Yes, they all had their own special way of showing their love. You'll have to remember that their love continues whether they're here or they are in Heaven.

I suppose I could get into those tiny details, like opening the door for women, changing the toilet paper roll, or bringing flowers home once in a while, but I have complete faith that you'll figure it all out. Your dad has always done a great job of preparing you to be gentlemen and hard workers. It will be up to you to choose other role models in your life. If you can remember the old saying *you are who you hang out with*, you'll see just how important it is to surround yourself with quality people and have great mentors. Spend time with people who honor your worth and celebrate your unique gifts. This reminds me—choose a partner that gives you butterflies and understands your heart and your core values. Remember, that we can show anyone how to make Salvadorian Turkey, but ultimately, I hope you find someone that makes you laugh, someone you can talk to about your tough day with, and someone that loves to be held in your arms while you're slow dancing. Oh yes, I hope you slow dance every chance you get.

I've always enjoyed having a puzzle to work on in the living room. In many ways I think it's a great analogy for life and connection. As you will see, life is about making all the colorful pieces fit together. Occasionally, you'll want to check to make sure that you still have all the pieces. That means coordinating all the important elements in your life: love, faith, purpose, and self consideration. Those are the four cornerstone pieces that seem to hold everything together. The great news is that you can do it your own unique way. You can turn over one piece at a time and then start the process, you can work on a colorful section that peaks your interest, or you can create some structured plan that begins with finding all the edges and work your way in. There's certainly no right or wrong way to do it. Life is an endless challenge of sorting, balancing, and reconfiguring your passion and priorities. You'll just have to remember that most things go in one piece at a time.

I don't mind telling you that this book started off one way and changed courses about half way through. You'll have to do that a lot in your life, shift gears, go to plan B or jump ship. It's all a part of the adventure. If you're unsure about a decision, talk about it with someone who has your back or pray about it. You're going to be great. I'll never forget the moment that I was waiting to hear if the publisher was going to accept my book proposal. Vince pulled me aside and said, "Mom, if it's not this publisher, then you'll just find another way to do it." I thought to myself, "How amazing that this twelve year old already understands that things don't always work out the way we want it to, and dreams are worth fighting for." Remember that your ideas and your goals are important, and your desire for greatness falls on your own courage and determination. Don't ever give up. Whatever it is, don't ever give up. Remember that fear of failure is not a good enough reason to sit on the sidelines. You are always stronger than you think. There were plenty of times in your life when I watched you play your heart out at a basketball game. Just do the same thing with life. Whether you're on the bench or on the court, be a positive team player. Practice sportsmanship, support the people around you, and show the world why you deserve to take the last shot at the buzzer.

If you start and finish your day with some prayer of gratitude, you will be blessed a hundred times over. You were born with everything you need. I believe that there's simply nothing that you cannot accomplish if you put your mind and heart into it. The rite of passage is a glorious adventure. Just remember that everything will come to you in its own perfect time. Trust your instincts and savor the moments. Just know that God has a special plan for you, and he entrusted you with one another. As brothers, take care of one another, show up for each other, and be that favorite uncle to your nieces and nephews. I suppose every mother hopes that she can give her children the best foundation for living. I hope you'll look back and say, "My mom looked for love everywhere. She found it in feathers, heart shaped rocks, and puffy clouds. She was passionate about bringing people together for no particular reason other than to love. She sang really loud in car, and *Wake Me Up* became an anthem for her life. It was her greatest calling

TO MY SONS

to become a mother and a peacemaker. She did everything possible to show up for life and teach us to live completely true to ourselves. Her greatest joy was watching us seek out ways to give and receive love. Yes, it was all she ever wanted."

I love you Frank.
I love my Vince.

Be Good.
Mama

ABOUT THE AUTHOR

Meet author and philanthropist, ***Krista Emma Gawronski***.

On most days you can find Krista with her husband at their little sandwich shop in Petaluma, California or she may be at the local basketball gym cheering on her two sons, Frank and Vince. She has always been busy and blessed. She decorates her life with family, friendships and a few disobedient dogs. It seems she couldn't ask for anything more —or could she?

Inspired by Oprah Winfrey and stimulated by her local community, she began longing for a greater purpose outside of herself. She placed her restless heart on her faith, and the Universe nudged her toward a philanthropic mission. With the love of her dearest Soul Sisters, The Fabulous Women of Sonoma County was born. This grassroots organization became a force of love in her community, and she started a bandwagon of kindness. Everyday people joined the movement and performed extraordinary acts of love. The group captured a huge audience and a platform to gather, give, exchange stories, help families in need, and support meaningful local causes.

Her passion grew and so did her desire to spread compassion and promote humanity. It became so great that she found herself restless again. She became focused on a larger dream, to spread a simple formula for giving throughout the nation. What came next would literally surprise her. The love and wisdom of her experience poured out of her and onto the pages and chapters of this book. *Soul Purpose* became her passion to raise the level of love and charity in the world. It is Krista's prayer and intention to turn community giving into a daily expression of our hearts, and she hopes that more charitable groups will pop up all over the country.

It is a Spirit that gathers on purpose and relies on human kindness. Could it be that this everyday mother and friend would find her peace and her purpose underneath her nose? If you ask her, the answer will be an emphatic YES! She believes that our journey to find grace and joy need not be far. It is already inside of us, and we are all just finding our own courage to fly.

Connect with Krista:
Email: info@kristagawronski.com
Facebook: www.facebook.com/soulpurpose16
Instagram: Soulpurposeandcharity
Or visit www.kristagawronski.com

A portion of the proceeds from **Soul Purpose** will support two charitable organizations.

> The first **The Fabulous Women of Sonoma County** which Krista helped start in 2005. The Fabulous Women have a program called "Gifts of the Heart" that helps families experiencing extraordinary hardships. To learn more about this philanthropic group, please visit **www.thefabulouswomen.com**.

> The second is **Alex's Lemonade Stand Foundation (ALSF).** The donation is a tribute to loved ones affected by cancer. By supporting ALSF we can raise hope for the future and fund research. To learn more about this amazing organization, visit their webpage: **www.alexslemonade.org**.

Made in the USA
San Bernardino, CA
03 March 2017